The Quest for Mark's Sources

The Quest for Mark's Sources

*An Exploration of the Case
for Mark's Use of First Corinthians*

Thomas P. Nelligan

PICKWICK *Publications* · Eugene, Oregon

THE QUEST FOR MARK'S SOURCES
An Exploration of the Case for Mark's Use of First Corinthians

Copyright © 2015 Thomas P. Nelligan. All rights reserved. Except for brief quotations in critical publications or reviews, no part of this book may be reproduced in any manner without prior written permission from the publisher. Write: Permissions, Wipf and Stock Publishers, 199 W. 8th Ave., Suite 3, Eugene, OR 97401.

Pickwick Publications
An Imprint of Wipf and Stock Publishers
199 W. 8th Ave., Suite 3
Eugene, OR 97401

www.wipfandstock.com

ISBN 13: 978-1-62564-716-0

Cataloging-in-Publication data:

Nelligan, Thomas P.

The quest for Mark's sources : an exploration of the case for Mark's use of First Corinthians / Thomas P. Nelligan.

xvi + 170 p. ; 23 cm. —Includes bibliographical references and indexes.

ISBN 13: 978-1-62564-716-0

1. Bible. Mark—Sources. 2. Bible. Mark—Relation to Corinthians, 1st. 3. Bible. Corinthians, 1st—Relation to Mark. I. Title.

BS2585.52 Q37 2015

Manufactured in the U.S.A.   07/06/2015

*Looking back I dedicate this book to the memories
of my grandfather and father.*

*Gordon 'Gig' Roche
Missed every day.*

*Michael Nelligan
Missed every second.*

*Looking forward I dedicate this book to my son Michael David Nelligan
and all the possibilities that the future holds.*

Contents

List of Tables | viii
Acknowledgments | ix
Abbreviations | xi
Introduction | xiii

1 Ancient Literary Methods of Text Absorption | 1
2 Criteria for Judging Literary Dependence | 18
3 Mark and Paul: A Brief History of Research | 33
4 First Corinthians and Mark: An Overview | 49
5 Comparison and Analysis of 1 Corinthians 1–2 and Mark 1:1–28 | 55
6 Comparison and Analysis of 1 Corinthians 5 and Mark 6:14–29 | 100
7 Comparison and Analysis of 1 Corinthians 11:2–34 and Mark 14:1–25 | 113

   Assessment and Conclusion | 148

Bibliography | 155
Subject Index | 163
Ancient Documents Index | 165

Tables

First Corinthians and Mark: An Overview | 53

First Corinthians 1–2 and Mark 1:1–28 | 59

First Corinthians 2 and Mark 1:21–28 | 91

First Corinthians 11:2–34 and Mark 14:1–25 | 119

Steps of the Eucharist in 1 Cor 11:23–26 and Mark 14:22–25 | 136–37

Acknowledgments

THIS BOOK REPRESENTS A highly revised version of my doctoral thesis which was written during the period of 2007–2011 at the Dominican Biblical Institute in Limerick, Ireland and presented to Mary Immaculate College in December of 2011.

There are so many people to thank that it is very hard to know where to start. Over the years I have been aided by some wonderful scholars and friends, and if I have left anybody out I apologise in advance.

Firstly, I must thank Dr. Christopher D. Stanley whose excellent tutoring in New Testament Greek gave me the necessary tools to complete this study. I also need to thank Dr. Regina Plunkett-Dowling and Dr. Adam Winn whose feedback and friendship have greatly enhanced my work. Special mention needs to be made of John Shelton and his wonderful wife Grace. Their friendship and support, given not just to me but to my family as well during some very dark days, have been a great source of joy.

I am eternally grateful to everyone who worked at the Dominican Biblical Institute during my time there. In particular Peig McGrath, Brendan Clifford, and Mary T. Brien deserve special mention for all their help and patience over, what could only be described as, a turbulent four years. Of course, guiding me all the way was my supervisor Dr. Thomas L. Brodie OP. Thank you for your patience, time, energy, and relentless hard work throughout this undertaking. I am extremely proud to have been your student.

Special mention also needs to be made of Dr. Jessie Rogers whose constructive criticisms have helped me grow as a scholar. Dr. Rogers has been a constant guide through the murky waters of scholarship. Dr. Wilfred Harrington OP also deserves thanks for his constructive criticisms which helped to shape the final form of this research. I would also like to thank

Acknowledgments

Dr. Douglas Estes and Joel L. Watts for all the advice they offered me when I first started to think about publishing this research and Pickwick Publications for accepting this work for publication.

Finally I would like to thank my wonderfully supportive and loving family who have been right behind me every step of the way. My grandmother and late grandfather have always been encouraging in every way and for this I am truly grateful. My amazing wife, Maria, has helped me in so many ways that I don't think I could have got to the end successfully without her love—her patience throughout seemingly endless revisions is truly astonishing. I will always be indebted to my mother who has, since my first day in undergraduate studies, meticulously proof-read everything and typed up endless notes, papers, and even drafts of this book. To her I owe the bulk of my appreciation. I admire your bravery and determined nature more than you will ever know. Lastly, I need to thank my late father who has, since as far back as I can remember, encouraged my love of learning. I am so glad that you lived long enough to see the first completed draft of the thesis on which this book is based. I wish you were here to see the rest—it never would have happened without your love and support.

Abbreviations

JOURNALS AND SERIES

AB	Anchor Bible
ABD	*Anchor Bible Dictionary*
BNTC	Black's New Testament Commentaries
BZNW	Beihefte zur Zeitschrist für die neutestamentliche Wissenschaft
CRINT	Compendia rerum iudaicarum as Novum Testamentum
DPL	*Dictionary of Paul and His Letters*
ErIsr	*Eretz-Israel*
JBC	*Jerome Biblical Commentary*
JBL	*Journal of Biblical Literature*
JSNT	*Journal for the Study of the New Testament*
JSNTSup	Journal for the Study of the New Testament: Supplement Series
LCL	Loeb Classical Library
NJBC	*New Jerome Biblical Commentary*
NovT	*Novum Testamentum*
NTS	New Testament Studies
RBL	Review of Biblical Literature
SBL	Society of Biblical Literature
SNTSU	Studien zum Neuen Testament und seiner Umwelt
SwJT	*Southwestern Journal of Theology*
UBS	United Bible Society
WUNT	Wissenschaftliche Untersuchungen zum Neuen Testament
ZNW	*Zeitschrift für die neutestamentliche Wissenschaft und die Kunde der älteren Kirche*

Abbreviations

GRECO-ROMAN, JEWISH, AND EARLY CHRISTIAN TEXTS

1 Clem.	Clement of Rome, *1 Clement*
Aen,	Virgil, *Aeneid*
Ag. soph.	Isocrates, *Against the Sophists*
Ant.	Josephus, *Jewish Antiquities*
Antid.	Isocrates, *Antidosis*
Ant. or.	Dionysius of Halicarnassus, *De Antiquis Oratoribus*
Argon.	Apollonius of Rhodes, *Argonautica*
Ars.	Horace, *Ars Poetica*
CD	*Damascus Document*
Cons.	Augustine, *De Consensu Evangelistarum*
Const. ap.	*Apostolic Constitutions*
Crass.	Plutarch, *Crassus*
De. Bel.	Lucan, *De Bello Civili*
De. or.	Cicero, *De Oratore*
Eph.	Ignatius, *Ephesians*
Fin.	Cicero, *De Finibus*
Haer.	Hippolytus, *Refutatio Omnium Haeresium*
Hist.	Herodotus, *The Histories*
Hist. eccl.	Eusebius, *Historica Ecclesiastica*
Hist. rom.	Livy, *History of Rome*
Il.	Homer, *Iliad*
Inst.	Quintilian, *Institutio Oratoria*
Inv.	Cicero, *De Inventione Rhetorica*
Jos. As.	*Joseph and Aseneth*
LXX	Septuagint
Od.	Homer, *Odyssey*
On Imit.	Dionysius of Halicarnassus, *On Imitation*
Opt. gen.	Cicero, *De Optimo Genere Oratorum*
Paneg.	Isocrates, *Panegyricus*
PGM	*Papyri Graecae Magicae*
Phil.	Polycarp, *Philemon*
Rom.	Ignatius, *Romans*

Introduction

IN THE CONTEXT OF Markan priority, identifying specific written sources for Mark has simply not been a priority for scholars. The "Two Source Hypothesis," generally accepted by Markan scholars and others alike, has ensured that Mark's sources remain a largely unexplored avenue. As Mark is considered to be a source for both Matthew and Luke, most research focuses on the use of Mark by the other gospel writers. The Church traditionally placed Mark's gospel second in composition, after Matthew, and this can be seen in the ordering of the New Testament today. This view, supported by Augustine,[1] was dominant until the end of the eighteenth century. However, during the nineteenth century, studies carried out by scholars such as C. G. Wilke and H. J. Holtzmann proposed that Mark was indeed written first and was used as a source by both Matthew and Luke.[2] This paved the way for the treatment of Mark in the next century. It became standard practice to view Mark as a collector of now lost written and oral traditions circulating in the decades following Jesus' death. In the early twentieth century, form criticism served to cement this view that Mark was a collector of traditions by focussing on its pre-literary phases.[3]

Redaction criticism reunited the text and argued that although there were traditions behind Mark, the author was creating a theologically unified document and was not merely stitching these traditions together.[4] In this view Mark becomes a loose combination of oral and written sources, none of which are extant, but exist in an altered form within the gospel,

---

1. Augustine, *Cons.* 1, 2 (4). Augustine said of Mark's relationship to Matthew: "Mark follows him closely and looks like his attendant and epitomizer."
2. Wilke, *Der Urevangelist*. Holtzmann, *Die synoptischen Evangelien*.
3. Telford, "Introduction," 6.
4. Ibid., 7.

Introduction

unified by the author's theological agenda.[5] Mark was at least granted some creativity.

Source criticism narrowed the field of possible sources for Mark and proposed that only a similar text could possibly be a source. The result of this narrow view of genre was the creation of hypothetical sources for Mark. Much has been written about these hypothetical sources such as "proto-Mark," "*Ur*-Mark," "Deutero-Mark," and the "secret Gospel of Mark."[6] These theories, while helpful, are unsatisfactory for explaining the composition of Mark as they rely on an unknown element.

What, then, is the result of this scholarship? Firstly, it has resulted in a large-scale disinterest in Markan sources. As Adam Winn has pointed out, a quick glance of the available commentaries on Matthew, Mark, and Luke will show this disinterest. In commentaries on Matthew and Luke, introductory sections dealing with sources are standard and expected. In commentaries on Mark, they are rarely present.[7] Secondly, Mark is viewed as somewhat clumsy in his presentation. Mark becomes an unoriginal, copy-and-paste writer who stitched together the written and oral traditions that were available to him. Mark may have stamped some form of theological agenda onto these sources, but they are still largely present in the canonical text. Lastly, it has resulted in large-scale group-think within biblical studies. Scholarship has been entrenched in this view of Mark meaning that new research that challenges this largely accepted view is eyed with suspicion with scholars ready to throw around terms such as "parallelomania."[8] Such discourse is not helpful. Change, when it comes, comes slowly.

However, change is in the air. The pioneering work of scholars such as William R. Telford, Joel Marcus, Thomas L. Brodie, Dennis R. MacDonald, and Adam Winn has strongly indicated that Mark was not a simple cut and paste writer but a skilled author perfectly capable of using sources. The work of Brodie, MacDonald, and Winn in particular has shown that not only was Mark comfortable with using sources, but also used sources that are still extant. The SBL Markan Literary Sources Seminar has given

---

5. See Marxsen, *Mark*. For a general discussion on redaction criticism see, Perrin, *What is Redaction Criticism?* Stein, "What is Redaktionsgeschichte?" 45–56. Rohde provides a review of redaction criticism in Markan studies, Rohde, *Rediscovering the Teaching*.

6. Crossan, *Four Other Gospels*. Fuchs, "Die Entwicklung," 139–47. Koester, "History and Development." Smith, *Secret Gospel*. Trocme, *Formation of the Gospel*.

7. Winn, *Elijah-Elisha*, 1.

8. The term parallelomania was coined by Samuel Sandmel who used it in his SBL address: Sandmel, "Parallelomania," 1–13.

Introduction

a platform to established and emerging scholars to discuss these potential sources such as the Elijah-Elisha narrative in 1 and 2 Kings and the letters of Paul.

This new wave of research has also shown that New Testament writers need to be understood more against the background of Greco-Roman literature. In particular, Greco-Roman theories of imitation have been explored and have shown that vocabulary links between texts are not always the key in determining literary dependence. Vocabulary links have long been the most important marker of literary dependence in biblical studies but this may not be the case. A growing awareness of the surrounding literary context has allowed scholars to properly assess the texts of the New Testament. The high level of Hellenism found in first century Palestine means that to ignore such techniques would be negligent. The time is ripe for the writings of the New Testament to be reassessed in light of such techniques. Literary borrowing was such a common-place practice in Greco-Roman literature, as we are informed by ancient texts, that we are at the beginning of a threshold in biblical studies that could very well see a radical reinterpretation of the texts.

For Mark, apart from the obvious use of the Old Testament, other extant sources have rarely been suggested until recently. The letters of Paul represent the earliest extant Christian texts pre-dating the earliest gospel. As well known, later Old Testament texts used earlier ones, it is fair to ask if later New Testament texts used earlier ones also. This idea has not been plucked out of thin air. From antiquity to the modern day there have been those who have connected Mark and Paul. Yet, the matter remains unsatisfactorily explored. Since the publication of Gustav Volkmar's *Die Religion Jesu* in 1857, which postulated that Mark was a Pauline gospel, little other work has been done on the issue apart from a handful of articles and the rare mention of a similarity in a commentary or monograph.[9] Mark's similarity to certain aspects of Paul has been ever present but never fully explored.

The purpose of the present study is to provide an in-depth comparison and analysis of sections of Mark with sections of the Pauline corpus in order to establish that Paul's letters, at the very least 1 Corinthians, were literary sources for the author of the Gospel of Mark. Thomas Brodie and Adam Winn have demonstrated effectively that the Elijah-Elisha narrative found in 1 and 2 Kings was a major source for Mark, and Dennis MacDonald has indicated that Mark may have also been drawing on the epics of

9. Volkmar, *Die Religion Jesu*.

Introduction

Homer. This study seeks to bring another component of Mark to the table by exploring the gospel's relationship to 1 Corinthians. First Corinthians represents a good starting point for research into this area as it has a wide subject matter and shares some common themes with the Gospel of Mark.

With this in mind, the present study will begin in chapter 1 with a discussion of Greco-Roman literary techniques. The purpose of this is to build a framework into which data from the later chapters can be understood and interpreted. Chapter two will delve into the methodology necessary to complete such a close analysis of two texts. Discussion of this is essential as this study proposes a new set of criteria for judging literary dependence through which data will be analyzed. Such criteria are essential for building and maintaining a credible case. The third chapter will analyze what previous scholarship has to say about the relationship between the Gospel of Mark and the letters of Paul. From here it will be possible to look closely at the texts. Chapter four will focus on the texts of Mark and 1 Corinthians and how they might relate to each other and what areas may prove fruitful for further analysis. Chapters five through seven will focus on specific areas of the texts. Portions of both Mark and 1 Corinthians will be compared and analyzed and the collected data will be viewed through the criteria for judging literary dependence. It is here that the case for Mark's use of 1 Corinthians will be built.

The answer is not an obvious one; if it were, it would already be known. Comparing texts that outwardly appear to have little in common can seem, on the surface, a potentially fruitless task. Yet, a close reading and analysis of portions of Mark and 1 Corinthians reveals several points of convergence that are consistent with ancient techniques of literary composition—particularly in relation to the use and transformation of sources. Mark emerges as a rich tapestry whose author skilfully wove together many sources in the creation of this gospel. One of these sources is 1 Corinthians.

— 1 —

Ancient Literary Methods of Text Absorption

INTRODUCTION

The texts speak for themselves, but for a modern reader to gain anything approaching a full understanding it is necessary to know something of the intellectual world in which they were written.¹

IN DISCUSSING ANCIENT LITERARY methods of text absorption it is necessary, as modern readers, to separate modern literature from the ancient as the understanding of modern literature and its composition may color knowledge and understanding of the ancient. The world of literature has drastically changed in the past centuries due in large measure to the invention of the alphabetic letterpress print in the fifteenth century and the publication of the French Encyclopaedia in the eighteenth century.² This saw a shift in the psyche of the literate mind. In the ancient world, knowledge was considered precious and was, therefore, preserved in written texts through the reuse of older texts.³ In the modern world knowledge has become much more readily available and the focus of literature has shifted towards originality and has become less focussed on preserving the written traditions of

---

1. Lambert, *Babylonian Wisdom*, 2.

2. Ong, *Rhetoric*, 276–78.

3. Ibid., 276–79; Brodie, *Birthing*, 3. See also Van Seters, *Edited Bible*, 15–18; and Derrenbacker, *Ancient Compositional Practices*, 30–44.

The Quest for Mark's Sources

the past. In fact: "No ancient text advocates or manifests sheer innovation."[4] Today, however, knowledge has become secure and is produced *en masse* and writers can focus on exploring the unknown and not on enshrining the "known" in literature.[5] In recent years the internet has made information and literature available at the click of a button in people's homes. Pen and paper, it seems are obsolete. This was not how the ancient world of literature conducted itself. There was no internet, no copyright laws and no printing presses. Everything had to be written by hand. This meant that the decision to put something down on paper was not one that was made lightly. Thus, the process of writing was complex and meticulous. Since all copies of texts had to be made by hand, it was easy for texts to become lost as not many copies of a text would have existed. Apart from making copies of older texts, one way in which a text could be preserved and transmitted was for it to be rewritten in the form of a new text. In fact, ". . .ancient literary theory deliberately discouraged independent invention of material."[6] Since subject matter was considered common property, there was no stigma attached to using the themes of an older text and incorporating it into a new text.[7] According to Robert Derrenbacker ". . .most Synoptic source-critical discussions take place without reference to the literary cultures of antiquity."[8] This study does not intend to make that mistake.

The Gospel of Mark reflects Judaism and the early Christian movement but is also set against the backdrop of the Roman occupation of Palestine in a period when the Middle-East was highly Hellenized. As Levine noted, ". . .contacts of Jews and Judaism with the Hellenistic-Roman world proved immensely fructifying and creative."[9] The Jewish religion and Scriptures provide a huge background culturally, literarily, and religiously to the narrative and composition of Mark's gospel. Yet at the same time Mark's gospel is composed in Greek which indicates that it is not meant entirely for a Jewish audience.[10] Therefore, both Jewish methods of composition

---

4. Brodie, *Birthing*, 3. See also Bowra, *Heroic Poetry*, 368–403. Lambert, *Babylonian Wisdom*, 2.

5. Ong, *Rhetoric*, 278.

6. Fiske, *Lucilius and Horace*, 40.

7. Ibid., 39.

8. Derrenbacker, *Ancient Compositional Practices*, 19.

9. Levine, *Judaism and Hellenism*, xi.

10. The explanation of certain Jewish practices indicates a non-Jewish or mixed audience. For example see 7:3–4. The translation of the Aramaic terms used also indicates this.

and those of the Greco-Roman world played their part in the composition of Mark.

IMITATION AND REWRITING

One of the main processes by which one text was absorbed into another in the Greco-Roman world was by μιμήσις/*imitatio* which means imitation. This process pervaded all ancient genres.[11] Modern readers must not confuse μιμήσις with plagiarism. In literary usage μιμήσις is somewhat of an umbrella term covering many aspects of literary composition. One thing it does not cover is word for word copying. This, when not cited, is plagiarism and is discouraged by many ancient authors.[12] In terms of writing, imitation began in the classroom. Isocrates, Quintilian, and Cicero argue that first and foremost a student must imitate his teacher.[13] The process of μιμήσις generally went through three basic steps. First, an author would select a source text or texts. Secondly, came the gestation period when an author would become suitably familiar with the source text for the purpose of the third stage which was the transformation of the source text in to the new text.[14] It is in the third stage that the various processes of μιμήσις were employed. An author would also be expected to be an avid reader in order to be familiar with the many texts of the ancient world.[15] For Quintilian, in particular, constant reading was very important to the process of imitation and he saw it as a prelude to the process.

> We must return to what we have read and reconsider it with care, while, just as we do not swallow our food until we have chewed it and reduced it almost to a state of liquefaction, to assist the process of digestion, so what we read must not be committed to the memory for subsequent imitation while it is still in a crude state, but must be softened and, if I may use the phrase, reduced to a pulp by frequent re-perusal. (Quintilian, *Inst.* 10.1.19)[16]

---

11. Fiske, *Lucilius and Horace*, 26. McKeon, "Literary Criticism," 3.

12. See Cicero, *Opt. gen.* 14; *Fin.* 3.4.15; Quintilian, *Inst.* 1.9.2; Horace, *Ars.* 133.

13. Isocrates, *Ag. Soph.* 17–18, *Antid.* 175, 301–3. Quintilian, *Inst.* 10.2.2–4. Cicero, *De or.* 2.21.89–90.

14 Finkelpearl, "Pagan Traditions," 78–90. Fiske, *Lucilius and Horace*, 44. O'Leary, *Matthew's Judaization*, 15. See also, Seneca, *Epistles* 84.3.7. Seneca uses the image of a bee making honey from various pollen to convey the process of literary imitation.

15. Brodie, *Birthing*, 6.

16. See also Horace, *Ars.* 268–69. Horace recommends reading night and day while

The Quest for Mark's Sources

Turning to the Jewish literary context there is a significant amount of overlap with Greco-Roman techniques. However, terminology for Jewish methods is plagued by lack of clear definition.[17] Terms such as rewritten Bible and midrash are like imitation in that they cover a wide range of techniques but are not clear cut techniques in their own right. The influence of Hellenism on Judaism in the first century C.E. needs to be recognized when dealing with techniques of text absorption as this helps to explain some of the similarities of technique.

> Judaism . . . by the time of the first century C.E. was thoroughly Hellenized, both in Palestine and especially in the Diaspora. Attempts to divide sharply the Jewish heritage of Christianity from the Greek heritage fail to recognize the degree of Hellenization already part of Jewish culture.[18]

The degree to which Judaism became Hellenized makes difficult the assessment of texts from the perspective of Jewish literary practices alone. By the Hellenistic period they had become so thoroughly meshed together that to treat them separately would be to provide an improper and incomplete study of a particular text. While discussing Paul's technique of citation Christopher Stanley claims that, ". . . direct exposure through daily contact with Greek society or indirect absorption via "Hellenistic" influences on Judaism could easily account for any similarities in practice."[19] Stanley later goes on to conclude that Greco-Roman and Jewish methods of citation are essentially the same and virtually indistinguishable.[20]

Recent research also indicates that Greco-Roman methods of text absorption were use in New Testament composition. Anne O'Leary shows that in Paul's discussion of idol food he reinterprets and essentially rewrites aspects of the Torah for the purposes of his own argument and displays

---

Dionysius of Halicarnassus saw reading as imparting style. See Dionysius of Halicarnassus, *On Imit.* Frag.6.

17. Stamps, "Use of the Old Testament," 15.

18. Tolbert, *Sowing the Gospel*, 37–38. See also the important work, Hengel, *Jews, Greeks and Barbarians*.

19. Stanley, *Paul*, 268.

20. Ibid., 337. Stanley demonstrates with examples from both the Greco-Roman world of literature as well as from Jewish texts that both have similar attitudes when it comes to quotations, with both sharing a huge amount of freedom and variety in their treatment of literary sources.

the same fluidity and freedom in his treatment of sources as Greco-Roman writers.[21]

THE TECHNIQUES OF IMITATION

While there are a plethora of techniques that could be discussed here, only the ones pertinent to later arguments will be discussed in any great detail. The relevance of this to the present study cannot be overstated. Any two ancient texts could, theoretically, be shown to contain similarities but similarities that conform to ancient literary techniques need to be examined. Many have noted similarities between the works of Paul and the Gospel of Mark but none have measured those points of convergence against the literary context from which the texts emerged.

The many techniques used in imitation can roughly be divided into three basic categories: interpretation, paraphrase, and inventive imitation. Interpretation (*interpretatio*) involved the conversion of poetry to prose and the translation of texts.[22] However, it is the techniques involved in the other two categories that concern us here.

The second category is *paraphrasis* or paraphrase which could vary widely and, depending on its application, could result in a text close to its source or far from it.[23] An echo of another text could be as little as a single word. This was actively encouraged so that when paraphrasing a source text it could be both compressed and expanded with a certain amount of literary freedom.

> ... they should begin by analysing each verse, then give its meaning in different language, and finally proceed to a free paraphrase in which they will be permitted now to abridge and now to embellish the original, so far as this may be done without losing the poet's meaning. (Quintilian, *Inst.* 1.9.2)

Quintilian's view of paraphrase seems to be similar to inventive imitation from which it is sometimes hard to distinguish.[24] While discussing imitation in oratory Isocrates says the following:

---

21. O'Leary, *Matthew's Judaization*, 58–88.
22. Ibid., 15.
23. Ibid. Fiske, *Lucilius and Horace*, 36–37.
24. O'Leary, *Matthew's Judaization*. 16.

The Quest for Mark's Sources

> Furthermore, if it were possible to present the same subject matter in one form and in no other, one might have reason to think it gratuitous to weary one's hearers by speaking again in the same manner as his predecessors; but since oratory is of such a nature that it is possible to discourse on the same subject matter in many different ways—to represent the great as lowly or invest the little with grandeur, to recount the things of old in a new manner or set forth events of recent date in an old fashion—it follows that one must not shun the subjects upon which others have spoken before, but must try to speak better than they. (Isocrates, *Paneg.* 7–8)

Paraphrase, then, appears as a wide ranging process that was similar in some respects to inventive imitation and sometimes overlapped with it. At the core of paraphrase is the notion that the essential meaning of the text is being imitated. Among the techniques used in paraphrase were variation and emulation. *Varatio* (variation) is part of paraphrase and is related to invention. Variation, essentially, is the practice of making changes to the original source material so that what is said is not said in the same way. This also avoids the possibility of plagiarism.[25] *Aemulatio* (emulation) was almost competitive in its nature.[26] Emulation was the practice of not only imitating a source text but aspiring to improve on it and create something that is greater than its predecessor.[27] Perfection was sought; Isocrates advised that writers abandon any area of literature in which perfection had been achieved and Roman writers would seek to emulate and surpass their Greek counterparts and predecessors.[28] This is connected to interpretation where translators would aim to surpass the original texts.

Turning to inventive imitation O'Leary, echoing Thomas Brodie, points out the similarities between paraphrase and inventive imitation: "It is not always easy to distinguish between methods of inventive imitation and paraphrase. In general, however, a paraphrase followed the broad outline of its source whereas inventive imitation treated it with far more creativity and in far greater detail."[29]

---

25. Fiske, *Lucilius and Horace*, 27. Fiske describes plagiarism as the wholesale copying from a source text where it is not cited and then presented as the writer's own work. He provides an example from ancient literature where Fidentius has copied and presented the poems of Martial as his own.

26. Brodie, *Birthing*, 7.

27. See Isocrates, *Paneg.* 7–8.

28. Ibid., 3–6.

29. O'Leary, *Matthew's Judaization*, 16.

It was not enough to just imitate the source—it had to become something new, with the addition of new material or by combining it with another source.[30] Being essentially a creative art, at the core of all literature is creativity, and therefore imitation, to some extent, serves this creativity.

> For there can be no doubt that in art no small portion of our task lies in imitation, since, although invention came first and is all-important, it is expedient to imitate whatever has been invented with success. And it is a universal rule of life that we should copy what we approve in others. (Quintilian, *Inst.*10.2.1–2)

What this serves to show is that there is no fixed formula to imitation as it is always second to creativity and invention. Creativity is fluid and allowances must be made for this as, to expect that all literature can be analyzed completely scientifically, is to treat literature as something fixed and not fluid. Inventive imitation, like the preceding categories covers a wide range of techniques.

A simple process was the adding of material to a text or omitting part of the source text which would not make sense in the new literary context. The technique of addition is sometimes known as elaboration.[31] Positivization and/or Negativization were the processes of taking something that was originally positive or negative in a source text and reversing it in its new literary context. Brodie provides a simple and helpful example of this process in Virgil's use of Homer. The negative anger of Achilleus in the *Iliad* is transformed and made positive in the devotedness of Aeneas to Dido in the *Aeneid*.[32]

Internalization was a somewhat more complex process and involves taking what was external and public in the source text and making it internal and private. The focus is usually on emotion and about the thoughts of the characters in a text. Amplification is the expansion of a source text through repetition and other techniques. This is closely related to addition and elaboration.[33] Contemporization is the simple process of updating a text to fit in with its new literary context, while universalization takes a quality or an aspect of a text and makes it universal. Virgil, for example, takes the stoic ideal of *pietas* and makes it a universal Roman ideal.[34]

30. Brodie, *Birthing*, 7.
31. Ibid., 10.
32. Ibid., 11.
33. O'Leary, *Matthew's Judaization*, 17n58.
34. Ibid., 17n60.

The Quest for Mark's Sources

Contaminatio (contamination) may suggest something negative but this is not the case. Contamination is the fusing together of many sources into a new text and was extremely common. For example, Virgil not only used Homer but also used the *Argonautica* of Apollonius Rhodius.[35] A writer would select many source texts and pick the best qualities from among them in creating a text.[36] Quintilian urged his students to use many models in order to the use the best qualities of each.[37]

Correctio (correction) is a simple technique where a writer would correct details of the source text. This was a common technique among historians.[38] Compression or synthesis is the combining of two or more scenes in a source text into one scene in its new literary context.[39] *Distributio* (distribution) is the dispersal of details from one scene in a source text to many places in the literary context.[40] Reversal is the simple technique of taking elements of the source texts and reversing them.

While ideas and themes can be imitated, quotation also forms part of μιμῆσις. Speaking of quotation techniques in the Greco-Roman literary world Christopher Stanley says that, ". . . the Greco-Roman writers . . . exhibit a high degree of flexibility and originality in the way they merge quotations into the developing flow of their own compositions."[41] This has the result that a writer could completely remove any indication that there is actually a quotation because the writer's own words and style have masked this.[42] Therefore, traces of a source text can be little more than the faintest allusion.

TECHNIQUES IN PRACTICE

It is not enough to merely list and describe the various techniques involved in imitation. Rather, a few examples will serve to show how certain

---

35. See Nelis, *Vergil's Aeneid*.

36. Brodie, *Birthing*, 7. Dionysius of Halicarnassus, *Ant. Or.* 4. Cicero, *Inv.* 2.1–5. Quintilian, *Inst.* 10.2.14–15; 10.1.108.

37. Quintilian, *Inst.* 10.2.24–6. See also, Nelis, *Vergil's Aeneid*, 4.

38. O'Leary, *Matthew's Judaization*, 18n62. For an example from Livy see Luce, *Livy*, 164.

39. O'Leary, *Matthew's Judaization*, 18n63.

40. Ibid., 18n65.

41. Stanley, *Paul*, 273.

42. Ibid., 274.

techniques were used. The examples used here will be limited to Virgil's imitation of Homeric texts and others, as this is, beyond a doubt, the most well recognised and widely studied example of ancient literary imitation.[43] It is important, not only because it involves some of the most influential texts to have come out of the ancient world but because Virgil blends multiple sources to create his epic (*contaminatio*). While Homer remains Virgil's major source throughout his epic, many other texts were used by the writer. The *Argonautica* of Apollonius Rhodius was another major source for Virgil. Works by Naevius and Ennius were also undoubtedly used but as these texts are now fragmentary their full influence and importance remains unknown.[44] Virgil would also have had access to Latin translations of Greek epics such as Livius Andronicus' *Odissea* and Varro Atacinus' *Argonautica*, however, these are now lost.[45] The style of the *Aeneid* is influenced by Callimachus. In fact, the epic has been described as ". . .Homeric in form, Callimachean in style."[46]

The boxing match in the fifth book of the *Aeneid* is a good example of Virgilian *contaminatio*.[47] The boxing match in *Aen.* 5:424ff, between Entellus and Dares, is heavily dependent on the boxing match between Epeois and Euryalos in *Il.* 23:653-99. In *Od.* 18:66ff, the boxing match between the disguised Odysseus and suitor Iros is also a source for Virgil. The boxing matches in both the *Iliad* and the *Odyssey* are brief affairs. Euryalos is knocked out with a single blow and Iros' jaw is shattered in a similar manner. The Virgilian boxing match is a much more drawn out affair with the match going back and forth until Entellus finally overcomes Dares. However, why does Virgil draw out the boxing match in contradiction to his Homeric sources? It is because of the presence of a third source in the form of the *Argonautica* of Apollonius Rhodius. Book 2:1-97 of the *Argonautica* recounts a brutal boxing match between Amycus and Polydeuces which results in the death of Amycus. This source accounts for much of the non-Homeric detail in Virgil's boxing match.

However, the boxing match in *Argon.* 2 is also largely based on *Il.* 23 and *Od.* 18. Apollonius Rhodius verbally alludes to Homer and distributes

---

43. For brief synopsis of Virgil's use of Homer see, Gransden, *Virgil*, 24-35.
44. Nelis, *Vergil's Aeneid*, 3.
45. Ibid.
46. Clausen, *Virgil's Aeneid*, 14.
47. Nelis provides a more in-depth analysis of this passage. See Nelis, *Vergil's Aeneid*, 8-21.

details of the Homeric texts throughout his own.[48] This creates a two-tier allusion whereby Virgil imitates both Apollonius Rhodius and also Apollonius Rhodius' sources.[49] Virgil, at times, favors one source over another. The added details of the boxing match show Virgil's preference for Apollonius Rhodius at that point, while the lessened brutality at the end of the boxing match, which does not result in death, shows a preference for the more sporting bouts found in the *Iliad* and the *Odyssey.*

Through *contaminatio* and *distributio* Virgil has created a scene thoroughly his own but reminiscent of both Homer and Apollonius Rhodius. While Virgil's text stands alone, a deeper and richer understanding of the text can only happen through recognising Virgil's models and the interactions between them.

A quick character study of Virgil's eponymous hero, Aeneas, should serve to show Virgil's blending of sources, both literary and non-literary, through μίμησις. The nature of Virgilian imitation was wide ranging as indicated by the blending of literary and non-literary sources.[50] Why are non-literary sources significant? It is important to keep non-literary sources in mind, particularly in the study of the Gospel of Mark, as literary sources cannot possibly account for every line of a text. In the case of Virgil, he uses the political situation of the day as inspiration. In the case of Mark, the person of Jesus is the base to which literary sources are melded to create the fantastical text we know today.

In creating his hero, Virgil combined Homeric characters and ideals with the ideals of Stoicism and Augustan propaganda—skilfully blending literary and non-literary sources. The result is a new form of a familiar character. In Aeneas both Achilleus and Odysseus can be seen as well as the stoic philosopher and the Emperor Augustus.

Virgil's starting point is the Homeric Trojan hero Aeneas. Although important to the *Iliad,* Aeneas is not one of the major characters. He has two important duels, one with Diomedes and one with Achilleus. From both he has to be rescued by his divine mother Aphrodite. One important detail is Poseidon's prophecy that the Trojan people would live on through Aeneas.

At the beginning of the *Aeneid,* Aeneas is the fully fledged Homeric hero and Virgil uses Odysseus as his literary model. In book 1 of the *Aeneid,*

48. Nelis, *Vergil's Aeneid,* 9.
49. Ibid., 5.
50. Ibid., 6.

Ancient Literary Methods of Text Absorption

Aeneas laments and wishes he had died at Troy in battle, which is based on Odysseus' lament in book five of the *Odyssey*. That the Virgilian text here relies upon the Homeric text is well established. In fact only lines 12–33, 257–96 and 657–94 in book one of the *Aeneid* do not rely upon the *Odyssey*.[51] Aeneas' first spoken lines, beginning in line 94, are taken from this portion of the *Odyssey* and the dialogue and action are firmly rooted in the *Od.* 5.[52] This is a typical example of Virgil's use of Homer and a clear case of imitation using techniques such as omission (Virgil condenses Odysseus' speech) and interpretation in his translation.

However, this example is but one small detail. On a larger scale both Aeneas and Odysseus share much more. Both have long sea journeys, are waylaid, and are pursued and aided by gods, showing large scale adaption of plot. In a reversal Odysseus is returning home while Aeneas is fleeing his home to establish a new one. Dramatic reversals are often used by Virgil in his use of Homer and he essentially reverses the entire Homeric plot of the *Iliad* and *Odyssey*. Not only is plot reversed but also themes, structure and character roles.[53] Yet at times Aeneas appears to be like Achilleus. During the sack of Troy, Aeneas is prepared to fight until death, which he knows will inevitably be the outcome. He chooses to fight for τιμή, and κλέος, two of the most important Homeric ideals. It is only through divine intervention that Aeneas finally leaves for Italy.[54]

As the epic progresses, Virgil uses other, and sometimes non-literary sources, as well as continuing to use Homer, to further the development of Aeneas from Homeric to Augustan hero. Through a series of trials during the story, which serve to develop Aeneas' moral character, Virgil places Stoic ideals at the core of Aeneas' character, such as justice, moderation, courage, and wisdom.[55] Although Aeneas fails many times in respect to these ideals,[56] after arriving in Italy they firmly become part of his moral fibre and character.[57] Virgil does, however, deviate from the ideal Stoic type.

---

51. Williams, *Aeneid*, 154.

52. Ibid., 168–69. See also Quinn, *Virgil's Aeneid*, 102–103.

53. For a larger discussion of the role of reversals in Virgil see Winn, *Elijah-Elisha*, 11–30.

54. Stahl, "Aeneas," 170.

55. Bowra, "Stoic Ideal," 204–17.

56. In respect to wisdom, during the sack of Troy, Aeneas forgets about his wife Creusa, (*Aen.* 2:768–95). Again, during the sack of Troy Aeneas shows little moderation (*Aen.* 2:567–87).

57. Bowra, "Stoic Ideal," 211.

The Quest for Mark's Sources

The final books of the *Aeneid* show Aeneas fighting with ferocity and anger, something which the Stoics firmly shunned.[58] Rather, Virgil is again appealing to his Homeric source and combining elements of a wrathful Achilleus with that of the Stoic Aeneas.[59]

Through contemporization Virgil makes some obvious connections to Augustus, particularly in the final books. Some of these connections seem to be justifying Augustus' actions by providing a mythical background for them. The most obvious connection is that just as Aeneas sought revenge against Turnus for the murder of Pallas (who had essentially become Aeneas' adopted son) so Augustus had sought revenge for the murder of his adopted father, Julius Caesar.[60] Revenge was not part of the Stoic ideal, thus Virgil alters it to suit the view of the Augustan circle which aimed to show Augustus and his actions in a favorable light.[61] A further and bloodier connection is the human sacrifices that Aeneas performs (*Aen.* 11:59–99). Augustus, too, is said to have performed human sacrifices at his adopted father's altar after the battle of Perusia in 40 B.C.E.[62] Thus, Virgil attempts to justify Augustus' actions through his epic.

While Virgil imitates the Homeric hero, he alters it, contemporizes it, and adds new material to create something entirely new, yet familiar as older texts have been preserved within in. This example shows how a text can be woven into the fabric of a new text so that the similarities are very clear but at the same time have become something different in their new literary context. Although Virgil has clearly imitated Homer in the creation of the *Aeneid*, he has created a thoroughly Roman epic and has glossed over Homeric details with his own distinct language and style.

Imitation pervaded all ancient literature and while the terminology is different when dealing with Jewish texts the methods are comparable and largely the same. The degree of Hellenization in the region in the first-century C.E. hardly makes this a surprise.

---

58. Bowra, "Stoic Ideal," 212.

59. For a discussion of Virgil's use of the Homeric character Achilleus in the formation of Aeneas, see Mackay, "Achilles," 87–92.

60. Bowra, "Stoic Ideal," 212.

61. Ibid.

62. Stahl, "Aeneas," 159.

Ancient Literary Methods of Text Absorption

JEWISH LITERARY METHODS

When dealing with a Jewish text that reuses elements of an older text the term rewritten Bible is often used.⁶³ A text that can be said to have reworked another would show a close connection to the source text in regard to theme, vocabulary and theology and essentially presents the source in a new way through rearrangement, conflation and supplementation.⁶⁴ For Vermes, Josephus's *Antiquities,* Jubilees, the *Liber Antiquitatum Biblicarum* of Pseudo-Philo, and the *Genesis Apocryphon* were all examples of rewritten Bible.⁶⁵ Sidnie White Crawford has questioned Vermes' term "rewritten bible" as the texts Vermes includes in his genre are diverse. Crawford questions whether or not there are many sub-genres to this technique.⁶⁶ However, all these texts have a common purpose. The purpose of the revision is exegetical, that is, to explain or interpret the original text for a new (presumably later) audience.⁶⁷

Rewritten texts tend to follow their source quite closely and replicate the order, subject and genre of the source texts. The term is an umbrella term and plagued by a lack of clear definition.⁶⁸ An example of rewritten Bible is the Chronicler's use of 1 and 2 Samuel and 1 and 2 Kings. The Chronicler does not stray far from the sources but creates a new text at the same time.⁶⁹

It is, however, similar to imitation in that texts get conflated, expanded, distilled and elements dispersed. Rewritten Bible overlaps with another Jewish technique, namely midrash. In fact, rewritten Bible is often seen as part of midrash.⁷⁰ "The imprecision of the definition arises from a failure to distinguish between literary techniques and literary genres. For in itself,

---

63. The term "rewritten Bible" was coined by Geza Vermes in 1961 when he identified late Second Temple texts as being of this form of interpretation. Vermes, "Bible Interpretation," 184–91.

64. Ibid., 185–88. See also, Crawford, *Rewriting Scripture,* 2–3.

65. Ibid., 3.

66. Ibid.

67. Ibid.

68. Ibid., 10–12. See also Fishbane, *Biblical Interpretation.* Alexander, "Retelling," 99–121. Alexander has contributed to the debate of what the defining elements consist of rewritten Bible. Brooke, "Rewritten Law," 31–40.

69. Crawford, *Rewriting Scripture,* 3. Crawford gives many in-depth examples of rewritten Bible from Qumran and Intertestamental Jewish literature.

70. Porton, "Midrash," 4:818–22.

adapting or rewriting biblical material does not constitute a genre, but a technique used in different genres."[71]

Like rewritten Bible, midrash involves working closely with a source, also lacks firm definition and can be somewhat of an umbrella term in nature. It is the commentary on another text within the context of a new text. First and Second Chronicles, mentioned as a form of rewritten Bible above, are also often called midrash.[72] Midrash is essentially the method used at Qumran and in Rabbinic literature but is often discussed as it helps to provide a backdrop to the literature of the New Testament and the literary context from which it grew.[73] There is also a huge overlap between the techniques of rewritten Bible, midrash and the Greco-Roman techniques discussed earlier.[74] The term and categories set out by scholars are largely inadequate, particularly when dealing with Jewish methods. Hays claimed that these categories simply do not have the power with which to probe adequately.[75] Why, however, are these terms plagued by a lack of clear definition in biblical studies? Studies of classical texts do not appear to be hampered by such basic issues. The answer could lie in the tendency of biblical scholars to get stuck in "group-think" which over-estimates the historicity of biblical texts and downplays their literary artistry. Far too much emphasis is placed on the historical Jesus and less on the literary Jesus.[76] However, the tide is turning.

LEVELS OF TEXT ABSORPTION

The different levels to which a text can be absorbed must also be taken into account. Methods can be used to different degrees in imitation and one

---

71. Dimmant, "Mikra," 402.

72. Porton, "Midrash," 819.

73. Ibid., 819–21. Neusner gives an overview of Rabbinic midrash. Neusner, *Judaism*, 15–29. For more on Rabbinic midrash see, Porton, *Understanding*. Strack and Stemberger, *Introduction*, 233–359. Stern, "Rabbinic Parable," 78–95. Harman and Budick, *Midrash*, 3–37.

74. See Stanley, *Paul*, 268. Anne O'Leary has also demonstrated quite effectively that Jewish literary methods were comparable to Greco-Roman techniques, even within the New Testament. See O'Leary, *Matthew's Judaization*, 58–88.

75. Hays, *Echoes*, 173.

76. This is not to say that issues pertaining to the historical Jesus are not important, as the literary Jesus is certainly a reflection of the historical Jesus.

Ancient Literary Methods of Text Absorption

may find, for example, that distillation can happen on a micro and a macro level and to different levels in particular instances.

Echo and allusion, among other terms, can be used to describe differing levels of literary imitation in ancient texts. These terms have been developed for this very purpose and, like the terms used to describe the methods of literary imitation, are derivative of observable practices in texts and are an aid to understanding as opposed to rigid categories into which all cases of literary borrowing can be squeezed. Ultimately the texts under question are artistic in nature and cannot, therefore, be subject to such rigidity.

However, as with methods of text absorption there is a lack of clear and precise terminology in regard to the differing levels of imitation. In recent years, more definition has emerged and Dennis R. MacDonald has created a taxonomy for terms that deal with the levels of imitation and in particular his own search for the "antetexts" of Mark and Luke-Acts.[77] It is this taxonomy that is adopted here.

- *Citation*—This category is somewhat self-explanatory and covers explicit quotations of another text. This can be divided into two-sub-categories of a quotation that is identified and one that is not.

- *Paraphrase*—This has already been discussed above and involves the author of a text producing the content of his or her source in his or her own words.[78] There appears to be a certain overlap between the methods and the levels of literary borrowing. While paraphrasing is listed as a method it also represents one of the levels of text absorption and can act in both capacities. While it is a method insofar as that is how a writer has treated a source, it also represents the middle ground between citation and reference.

- *References*—This is a reference to a source text without an explicit citation or paraphrasing.[79]

- *Allusion*—Allusion is similar to a reference but is not explicit in nature, and is rather implicit, and may not always be readily visible. Like citation, allusion can fall into two categories; conforming and transforming. A conforming allusion does not go against its literary predecessor and uses it as part of an appeal. A transforming allusion goes against the

---

77. MacDonald, "Categorization," 211–25.
78. Ibid.
79. Ibid.

source and uses it in order to show the superiority of the new text being written. Most New Testament allusions fall into the former category.[80]

- *Echo*—An echo is a step down from an allusion and is again implicit in nature. An echo may only be recognisable from a common word or phrase.[81]

- *Redaction*—Redaction is concerned with what various writers did to material they used and is somewhat of an umbrella term that covers various techniques but like allusion these can be conforming or transforming in nature.[82]

- *Imitation*—Like redaction, this is an umbrella term and has already been dealt with extensively in this chapter. Imitation involved the use of a literary model in the creation of a new text and, again, can be conforming or transforming in nature.[83] Hays, following on from Greene,[84] has identified four rough sub-categories of literary imitation in regard to the New Testament. These are as follows:

  1. *Sacramental imitation*—Also known as "reproductive imitation," this technique involves an almost verbatim imitation which Hays terms as being "slavish."[85]

  2. *Eclectic imitation*—Also known as "exploitative imitation," this technique involves the mingling together of many different sources without binding to one in particular.[86]

  3. *Heuristic imitation*—This technique involves a heavy reliance on one particular source but unlike sacramental imitation it is not slavish in nature and the source text is modernized and altered to fit into its new literary context. The distance between the source and new text can be significant yet recognisable.[87]

---

80. Ibid.

81. Ibid. Hays' work on echoes in Paul provides some of the best evidence available of this technique at work within the New Testament. See in particular, Hays, *Echoes*, 34–83.

82. Ibid. Redaction, more than any other category has an important history within biblical scholarship. For a history of redaction criticism within biblical studies see, Van Seters, *Edited Bible*, 244–97.

83. Ibid.

84. Greene, *Light in Troy*.

85. Hays, *Echoes*, 173.

86. Ibid.

87. Ibid.

4. *Dialectical imitation*—Here the source text creates a form of contrast within its new context and this causes both to become vulnerable to criticism and interpretation by the other.[88]

The methods of text absorption noted earlier in the chapter must be understood in terms of the level of literary dependency being claimed. The question is not only how did one text use another but also to what extent?

CONCLUSION

What immediately becomes apparent from the above study is that there is a huge amount of fluidity in the way ancient writers in the Greco-Roman and Jewish world treated their sources and their absorption into a new literary context.[89] The terminology adopted by modern scholars is only one way to attempt to make sense of these various techniques. The texts being analyzed are artistic ventures and should be treated as such, and it must be accepted that not every text and not every case of literary dependence will fit into a neat box with a label. Rather these labels are an aid to understanding and are not strict categories. What also became apparent is that these terms are somewhat insufficient in their nature.

---

88. Ibid.
89. Steiner claims this fluidity to be limitless in scope. Steiner, *After Babel*, 424–25.

— 2 —

Criteria for Judging Literary Dependence

INTRODUCTION

Sometimes the echo will be so loud that only the dullest or most ignorant reader could miss it . . . other times there will be room for serious differences of opinion about whether a particular phrase should be heard as an echo of a prior text and, if so, how it should be understood.[1]

CRITERIA FOR JUDGING LITERARY dependence have been developed as a way to provide a checklist against which claims of literary borrowing can be measured. With no such criteria there is no limit to the claims that can be made. Beyond this they also provide a way to measure a claim's validity and assess its strengths and weaknesses in the effort to decide whether one text can be described as being dependent on another. How this is done has differed from scholar to scholar and no matter how meticulous the criteria are, the data is always open to interpretation and it should always be remembered that scholars are dealing with literature which, by its very nature, is subject to differing viewpoints. The criteria should, rather, be viewed as an aid to understanding as opposed to a rigorous set of rules that can be imposed on a text.

We are so far removed in time and culture from first century New Testament writers that such criteria becomes necessary in judging cases of literary dependence accurately. It is not enough to ask whether an allusion

---

1. Hays, *Echoes*, 29.

or echo makes sense to us, but rather did it make sense to its original audience. Nor can we say with any confidence that modern scholarship can detect every parallel between texts successfully. "Parallels can be phantoms."[2] They certainly can be phantoms to the modern reader and scholar and it must be remembered that texts often work on two levels. A text can be read at face value and still make sense to the reader. At another level those who can recognize all the allusions within a text get a much richer reading and understanding of it. If an allusion is easily missed it does not mean it is not possibly meant to be there but rather that the reader may not be familiar enough with the source text to make that recognition.[3] For the modern reader it can often come down to being raised in a completely different literary culture where the rules and techniques of ancient literature no longer apply. Our knowledge will always remain fragmentary. This is why criteria are important as they provide the scholar with the tools to detect what might ordinarily be missed.

PREVIOUSLY ESTABLISHED CRITERIA

While many sets of criteria have been developed over the past thirty years in New Testament scholarship, only the criteria of Richard Hays, Thomas Brodie, Dennis MacDonald, Dale Allison, and Outi Leppä will be discussed as these all represent a significant shift in the development of criteria for judging literary dependence.

Richard B. Hays developed seven "tests" for judging literary dependence and these are tailored for Paul's use of the Jewish Scriptures.[4] These tests are as follows:

- Availability—This test asks whether or not Paul had access to the Jewish Scriptures.[5]
- Volume—This test looks at the repetition of words and syntactical patterns within a proposed echo and also at the prominence of the passage being echoed within its original text. The test also looks at how much emphasis is placed on the echo in its new literary context.[6]

---

2. Allison, *Intertextual Jesus*, 3.
3. Ibid., 4.
4. Hays, *Echoes*, 29–32.
5. Ibid., 29.
6. Ibid., 30.

- Recurrence—This test looks to see how often Paul echoes a particular passage. For Hays, the more he seems to echo the same passage the stronger the case.[7]
- Thematic coherence—This examines how an echo fits into Paul's argument and thematic structure.[8]
- Historical plausibility—This is a test of the modern interpreter. This test asks whether or not the hearer/reader of Paul would have understood the scriptural echo. The object of this test is to make sure the modern scholar is trying to think from the first century C.E. perspective and not to interpret Paul, accidentally, as a Lutheran or deconstructionist, for example.[9]
- History of interpretation—Explores whether the echo has been noted before by modern or ancient commentators.[10]
- Satisfaction—Does the proposed reading make sense?[11]

Thomas L. Brodie's criteria developed over many works to their fullest form in the *Birthing of the New Testament*.[12] The context for these criteria is the exploration of the intertextuality of the New Testament while proposing a hypothetical gospel source, *Proto-Luke*. The criteria are divided into two main categories: "positive criteria" and "principles that can mislead." The positive criteria are divided into three sub-sections as follows:

a) External plausibility (Context)—This is similar to Hays' availability criterion.

b) Significant similarities—This consists of seven forms of similarity:

   1. Similarity of theme.
   2. Pivotal leads or clues—While a connection may not be obvious, the writer may include some pivotal clues indicating the source being used.
   3. Similarity of action and/or plot.
   4. Complete absorption of a text—This criterion basically asks if all of a text is absorbed or if parts are missing.

---

7. Ibid.
8. Ibid.
9. Hays, *Echoes*, 30–31
10. Ibid., 31.
11. Ibid., 31–32.
12. For Brodie's earlier criteria see Brodie, *Genesis*, 421–32 and *Quest*, 63–66.

Criteria for Judging Literary Dependence

5. Similarity of order.

6. Similarity of linguistic details—What vocabulary is shared and is it grammatically similar?

7. Complex coherence—If the absorption of a text is particularly complex, is it coherent and intelligible?

c) Intelligibility of the differences—This criterion argues that if a text differs from its source text then that does not mean they are not connected, rather the differences need to be intelligible. What reasons does a writer have in changing the source text? This criterion is important if there are many differences between the text and its source.

These are all important but no single one of the above can determine a case for literary dependence but rather multiple areas need to be satisfied and need to interact with each other in some manner such as common action/plot and order based around common themes and vocabulary. The significant similarities are a more complex form of Hays' volume, recurrence, and thematic criteria.

When dealing with his "principles that can mislead," Brodie lists six objections frequently made against literary dependence. Brodie argues that these have to be taken seriously but if not examined critically they can turn into principles that mislead. The six objections are as follows:

a) Some connections are weak—A case for literary dependence ". . . depends not on the weakest link, but on a whole series of links forming a chain. That some are weak does not matter as long as there are enough that are strong."[13]

b) The differences preclude dependence and point to a shared tradition.

> This is possible and cannot be directly disproved. But it is a gratuitous claim and cannot be proved. And since it bears the burden of proof—it claims documents that no one has ever seen or traditions for which there is no reliable evidence—it is in the weaker position.[14]

c) The similarities may be due to general familiarity rather than direct dependence.

d) The similarity does not conform to a particular literary model, therefore, there is no connection.

---

13. Ibid.
14. Brodie, *Birthing*, 47.

The Quest for Mark's Sources

e) Complex structures do not presuppose literary usage.

f) The similarity is due to oral tradition.[15]

The elements of Brodie's criteria are wide ranging and cover theme, action, plot, completeness, order, linguistic details and complex coherence. Beyond this the criteria try to make sense of the collected data and then attempts to eliminate other possibilities.

The context for Dennis R. MacDonald's criteria is the search for connections between the Gospel of Mark and Homeric epics of the *Iliad* and *Odyssey*. This is against the background of Greco-Roman methods of imitation. The criteria are as follows:

- Accessibility—This is the same as Hays' availability.
- Analogy—This looks at how one writer uses another and asks if other writers used the same text in the same way.[16]
- Density—This criterion looks at the volume of contacts between the two texts.[17]
- Order—Common order can greatly enhance a case for literary dependence but cannot, on its own, determine the issue.
- Distinctiveness—This revolves around what is unique to the two texts. Finding a rare word only used by two texts, for instance, increases the chances of literary dependency.[18]
- Interpretability—This criterion asks whether or not the way one text uses another is intelligible and asks why a writer chose to use a particular text.

Dale C. Allison's criteria are different yet again.[19] As opposed to the criteria of Brodie, MacDonald, and Hays, Allison trims his criteria down to three:

- History of interpretation—Have many commentators seen a particular connection between the two texts?
- Shared elements—Do the texts share common elements such as vocabulary, word order, theme, imagery, structure and circumstances, and are these similarities unique to these two texts?

---

15. These criteria, as out lined by Brodie, are discussed in greater detail in *Birthing*, 43–49.

16. Ibid.

17. Ibid.

18. MacDonald, *Homeric Epics*, 8–9.

19. Allison, *Intertextual Jesus*, 10–13.

Criteria for Judging Literary Dependence

- Prominence of the source text—How prominent was the source text during the period in which it was being used?[20]

The criteria of Outi Leppä are unusual in that they allow for verbatim connections only. Drawing heavily on the word of E. P. Sanders,[21] Leppä has developed a set of criteria quite distinct from those put forward by Brodie, MacDonald, Hays, and Allison. The context of these criteria is the search for pseudepigraphal authorship of the disputed letters of Paul, particularly Colossians. Her work is based on verbal similarities between the two texts.

> . . . the agreement of two or three words can reveal literary dependence. Sometimes also the occurrence of three common words can indicate literary dependence in cases where it is exceptional that the words appear together.[22]

This is the basic notion that underlies the criteria that Leppä uses throughout the study. Excluded from this are stock phrases and common Pauline phrases which do not indicate literary dependence. Shared words have to be unusual enough to merit a case for dependence. More common words can indicate dependence but they have to be clustered together, therefore making it an unusual collection of vocabulary.

In the comparison of two similar texts the results can fall into one of three categories depending on the degree of verbal similarity. Each category then has certain criteria which the parallel must satisfy to be considered part of that category. These are as follows:

- Probable literary dependence—For Leppä there is probable literary dependence if there are more than three words shared by both texts and grouped together within a five line piece of text. The case is made stronger if these words are uncommon.
- Possible literary dependence—This is likely if there are three shared words grouped together in a five line piece of text. If the shared vocabulary is more commonplace then it would also fall into this category.
- The use of a similar style—Again, Leppä looks for three shared words within a five line context but if the words are very common in the early Christian world then the similarity can be ascribed to the use of a similar

---

20. Ibid.
21. Sanders, "Literary Dependence," 28–45.
22. Leppä, *Making*, 56.

style. These shared common words would not be highly related within their literary context.[23]

What is particularly interesting is that Leppä does not allow for anything other than significant agreement in vocabulary. Similarity in theme, motif, plot, or theology cannot, for Leppä, be indicators of literary dependence and she explains these similarities by saying that the two texts belong to a common tradition and culture. However, Leppä is quick to point out that her criteria are suited to the texts she is comparing, and that each case is individual and should be treated so.

> It is worth noting that the parallel texts cannot be compared with each other like weights or lengths of physical objects. The classification into three groups is only an approximation: every case has to be estimated individually.[24]

Two other sets of criteria deserve to be mentioned here but are not analyzed in full as they are similar to criteria discussed above. The first is a set of criteria presented by Anne. M. O'Leary. The context for her criteria is Matthew's Judaization of Mark's gospel. While they are solid and serve her study well, they are heavily dependent on the criteria of Hays, Allison, Brodie and MacDonald among others.[25] The same can be said about the second set of criteria, presented by Adam Winn, which are largely derived from both Brodie and MacDonald. However, Winn's criteria highlight the importance of awareness of Greco-Roman literary techniques. They also emphasize that vocabulary links are not always the most important marker of literary dependence.[26]

ANALYSIS OF PREVIOUSLY ESTABLISHED CRITERIA

While the above criteria are all significant and useful, there are certain criticisms that must be discussed before proposing new criteria. Hays' criteria are important because not only do they provide tests which a claim of a literary echo must pass, but they also provide tests which limit the scholar's own presuppositions when approaching the text which is essential in the on-going search for objectivity. However, these tests are somewhat

---

23. Leppä, *Making*, 53–58.
24. Ibid., 58.
25. O'Leary, *Matthew's Judaization*, 18–24.
26. Winn, *Elijah-Elisha*, 30–33.

Criteria for Judging Literary Dependence

basic and do not delve too deeply into questions of vocabulary, theme and theology.

Brodie's criteria lack any discussion of literary techniques, something which he spends great length discussing elsewhere.[27] It is puzzling as to why these were left out as rooting the criteria firmly in ancient literary techniques would have further strengthened his criteria. A second point of criticism of Brodie's criteria is that during the analysis of texts when the possibility of dependence of one text on another arises, the criteria are not explicitly applied. Without rigorous application the criteria are not as effective as they could be in assessing data that has been collected. However, Brodie has developed the criteria for judging literary dependence to a new, more detailed level. These criteria, when applied, provide a thorough test for any case of literary dependence.

One final criticism of Brodie's criteria concerns the negative criteria as principles that can mislead. While Brodie is correct to raise potential objections to a proposed case for dependence, these criteria have the effect of dismissing these possibilities rather than engaging with them. A case for literary dependence, therefore, becomes invulnerable to attack. Other explanations for collected data must be considered and engaged with for the sake of the rigour of the argument.

MacDonald's criteria, while significant, do contain certain flaws. Interestingly, vocabulary and plot do not factor amongst these criteria. MacDonald has chosen to focus on finding precedence in his analogy criteria to see if there are other texts that might relate to each other in a similar way. The criteria of density and order are more concerned with aspects of large scale borrowing on the macro level than they are with minute textual details on the micro level. Therefore, these are a very particular set of criteria for a particular purpose and they may not suit other texts or even other Markan sources. As is the case with all criteria, they are guides and do not prove anything conclusively. MacDonald points out these criteria ". . . are tests, not laws."[28] MacDonald's criteria are important in that they set tests for large scale macro literary borrowing and allow scholars to outline the possible usage of one text upon another before searching for more detailed information. However, this advantage is also a weakness in that this set of criteria lacks any criterion for vocabulary and aspects such as theme and theology, which, while not expected, would aid the scholar in understand-

---

27. Brodie, *Birthing*, 3–31.
28. MacDonald, *Homeric Epics*, 8.

The Quest for Mark's Sources

ing the nature of the relationship between the two texts and see the level to which literary borrowing may have occurred.

Turning to Dale Allison's criteria they are essentially a condensed version of Brodie's, MacDonald's, and Hays'. Both the "history of interpretation" and the "prominence of the source text" are similar to Brodie's "external plausibility," MacDonald's "accessibility" and "analogy," and Hays' "availability" and "history of interpretation." The "shared elements" criterion is, of course, common to all the sets of criteria and is the heart of them also. While other scholars have opted to have separate criteria for elements such as vocabulary, theme and circumstances, Allison has kept these together. While Allison's criteria are clear and concise they do not seem to recognize the effect these different elements can have. For example, two texts can share much thematically but very little in terms of vocabulary and vice versa. If Allison's criteria were to be used it might seem as if two texts were not connected if they were not to share certain thematic or vocabulary links. They may share a lot of imagery and structure but this would appear weak when measured against a lack of shared vocabulary. By separating these elements into different criteria it is possible to draw out the shared elements and view them individually before analyzing the full set of connections.

Leppä's is the only approach examined which does not allow for anything other than shared vocabulary as evidence for literary dependence. The criteria do not allow for similarities of theme, motif, plot, and theology as evidence for literary dependence. To only focus on vocabulary is to only focus on one aspect of the text. While Leppä's criteria may seem to lack in certain areas, as has been noted, it does have many positive aspects. Firstly, Leppä recognizes that the criteria cannot be used to prove literary dependence but only to aid in recognising the possibilities. Secondly, Leppä recognizes that each case needs to be judged independently and that the three categories in these criteria are suited to her own particular study. Finally, Leppä's criteria highlight the importance of shared vocabulary and this can aid scholars in analyzing shared vocabulary when it is found.

ESTABLISHING NEW CRITERIA

In establishing a new set of criteria certain elements need to be treated as flexible and others as a core to any set. In order to make investigations more rigorous the criteria should arise from what ancient writers were doing and

Criteria for Judging Literary Dependence

be driven by scholarly need to construct a credible and convincing case for literary dependence.

There are certain criteria that must be satisfied for any case of literary dependence to be made. These include criteria of date and accessibility. If, for example, text A cannot be shown to predate text B then text B cannot be dependent upon text A. Similarly, if it was absolutely impossible that text B could have had access to text A then a case for dependence cannot be made. Other criteria, while important, are not so integral to a case for dependence. While elements such as theme, vocabulary, order and completeness should be considered, no single one of these on its own is likely to prove a case for dependence and neither will each of these criteria be satisfied to the same degree. Also, if one criterion is not satisfied and all the others are then a case can still be made. The application of these criteria must be consistent and systematic in order to yield the best results. Although many have suggested criteria, they were not always applied throughout their respective studies. In order for the full effect of the criteria to be seen, the collected data of any investigation of literary dependence needs to be analyzed through the criteria.

The criteria being proposed here are outlined below and have a three part structure:

A External Criteria.
   1. Date
   2. Accessibility
   3. Status of the text
   4. Other uses of the source text

B Internal Criteria.
   1. Similarities of context, theme, action/plot, order, and completeness
   2. Common vocabulary
   3. Literary convention being employed and level of absorption
   4. Intelligibility/interpretability of the differences

C Probing Criteria
   1. Strong and weak connections
   2. Similarities due to a common tradition
   3. Similarities due to a general familiarity of the source text
   4. Redundancy

The Quest for Mark's Sources

Section A is basically common sense. It merely establishes the validity of asking the question, did text A use text B? Is this historically possible? How accessible was text B to text A? How well known was text B? Did other writers use text B? Date and accessibility are obviously essential to the argument. If the texts cannot pass these two criteria then further argument is invalid.

Date can also be a cloudy issue in certain instances. Mark 1:10 contains the unusual phrase σχιζομένους τούς ούρανούς which is not found anywhere else in the LXX or the New Testament. A similar phrase, however, is found in the text of *Jos.As.* 14:1–3 where the heavens are ripped apart and an angel descends to Aseneth. Is it possible that this text provides a source for Mark at this point?

For the purpose of this example the common post-70 date for Mark will be used. Dating *Joseph and Aseneth* is a difficult task with many dates being proposed. However, at best, a range of dates can be given between ca. 100 B.C.E. and ca. 115 C.E.[29] Therefore, a case of literary dependence is hard to proceed with as influence, if indeed there is influence, could be in either direction. The date criterion shows that proceeding with a case of dependence is hazardous as any conclusions reached would need to make an assumption about the dating of *Joseph and Aseneth*. While proceeding with the criteria would be useful, it would need to be carried out in both directions for a full argument to be presented.

The status and other uses of the source text are not essential to the argument but can obviously enhance it greatly. If text B was widely known and often used as a source text then it is more likely that it was known and used by text A. However, the "status of the text" criterion can be misleading and its importance can be overestimated. Showing that a text such as Genesis or any Old Testament text, for example, was well known is not a difficult task. In the case of Old Testament texts this criterion almost becomes redundant as these texts were so foundational in Jewish culture that there is no need to argue that they were well known. The same can be applied to the "other uses of the source text" criterion. With foundational texts such as the Hebrew Bible it is almost pointless to show other examples of its use as they are almost ubiquitous texts. Therefore, these latter two criteria of the external section need to be used with some caution.

The internal criteria consist of probing the texts in close detail. Elements such as context, theme, action/plot, order, vocabulary, and

---

29. Chesnutt, *From Death to Life*, 85.

completeness need to be examined. There is a certain amount of overlap between theme and action/plot. Whereas a theme can be general in nature, action/plot can be a chain of themes revealing a similarity of the events in both texts. Completeness will assess whether or not all the major elements of the source text are represented in the new text.

The issue of the role of vocabulary is one that requires discussion. What role does it play? Leppä's criteria only allowed for vocabulary links in a case for literary dependence. This, however, is far too narrow to assess the possibility that one text may be using another. Virgil's use of Homer has long been recognized yet Virgil composed in Latin while Homer was written in Greek. There is, therefore, no verbal agreement between the two, except in translation. Therefore, there is sometimes too much emphasis placed on vocabulary links. Although shared vocabulary can only serve to strengthen an argument of literary dependence, it is not always present. Not all techniques of text absorption require shared vocabulary. Therefore, it cannot be expected to be found in every case. This is particularly applicable in cases of dependence that cross genres where the language of one genre is not always applicable in another. New Testament studies have long placed too much emphasis on vocabulary links. Winn has highlighted this problem describing New Testament studies as ". . . a field that for far too long has operated under the false assumption that verbal agreement and verbal agreement alone is necessary to establish literary dependence."[30] Studies of classical texts do not appear to be hampered with an over-reliance on verbal agreements. An example will serve to illustrate this and how vocabulary links can be reconsidered in New Testament studies.

An example from Lucan who often alludes to Virgil's *Aeneid* will serve to highlight that vocabulary is not always the most significant marker when assessing literary dependence. Lucan in his *De Bello Civili* writes of Pompey's corpse:

> Hunc ego, fluminea deformis truncus barena qui iacet, agnosco.
> . . . Him I recognize, that disfigured trunk lying upon the river sands. (*De.bel.* 1.685–6)

This has long been recognized as an allusion to Virgil's description of the mutilated corpse of Priam in the second book of the Aeneid.[31] Virgil writes:

---

30. Winn, *Elijah-Elisha*, 32.
31. Hinds, *Allusion and Intertext*, 8.

The Quest for Mark's Sources

> . . . iacet ignens litore truncus, avulsumpue umeris caput et sine nomine corpus. . . . He lies a mighty trunk upon the shore, the head torn from the shoulders, a nameless corpse. (*Aen.* 3.557–8)

Only one word, *truncus,* is shared by the two yet the allusion remains. Furthering the connection between the two is that Virgil, while describing Priam is also alluding to the body of Pompey. This was commented upon in Servius' commentary on *Aen.* 2.557–8.[32] Therefore, Lucan, writing of Pompey, is alluding to Virgil's description of Priam which in itself is referring to Pompey. Underlying both texts is an historical event which shaped these texts which relate to each other intertextually. Vocabulary is not the main factor in this allusion; rather it is the reference to Pompey. While vocabulary remains important it should not be viewed as the marker by which all cases of literary dependence are judged.

The vocabulary criterion as described here allows vocabulary to remain important but does not view it as the deciding factor. Shared vocabulary is not always present and to assume that vocabulary is the only indicator of dependence is to vastly misunderstand how ancient writers composed their texts and handled their sources. New Testament studies need to reassess how it views the use of sources and should not shy away from proposing possible sources for fear of undermining the historicity of the texts. Even within this criterion there are degrees to which vocabulary is important. The presence of shared words is a valuable indication of dependence. However, if the words are extremely common then a case is weakened. If the shared words are less common or rare then a case is greatly enhanced. Added to this are issues of syntax and grammar. If a rare word is found in the same form in both texts then dependence is more likely. If other shared words can be found clustered around this then the case is further strengthened. If a common theme or plot can be added to this, then a valid case can surely be presented.

Absent from other criteria but included here is a criterion for identifying the literary convention being employed. What method of text absorption is being used, if any? The aim of this is to establish how one text is using the other, so that the process of textual absorption between the texts can be understood. Added to this is a criterion for judging the degree of dependence, if any. To what extent are the two texts connected? This involves levels of dependency such as allusion, echo, and imitation. The final criterion of section B discusses the differences between the texts.

32. Ibid., 9.

Can the differences be understood? This is largely adapted from the criteria developed by Brodie and MacDonald. This is not an essential criterion as differences do not preclude dependence.[33] If a text was not different then it would just be a copy. However, the discussion of differences can help to bring out how one text uses another and why the author uses the text in a particular way.

Section C is largely adapted from Brodie's criteria. However, in Brodie's criteria these were labelled as "principles that can mislead," while here they are labelled as "probing criteria" and are not approached from the same perspective. The effect of Brodie's "principles that can mislead" was not a probing of possibilities other than literary dependence but rather had the inadvertent effect of dismissing these possibilities. The "probing criteria" presented here are designed to explore alternate theories that could explain the similarities noted and to engage with the effect that weak connections have on the overall case. While appealing to common and unknown sources is problematic, it is a possibility that must be engaged with when assessing a case for literary dependence. While these texts were not written in isolation they form part of a larger literary culture in which authors had access to the same texts and techniques. Therefore, it would not be at all uncommon to find texts that are similar because they come from the same literary background. This criterion is, therefore, extremely important for that very reason. We need to be aware of this at all times and construct a credible argument that relies on evidence that points to a deliberate use of the source text.[34]

The final criterion in section C is entitled "redundancy." This criterion explores the possibility that another source can account for the data in a more satisfactory way. This criterion is not employed by other scholars and is designed to ensure that the relationship between multiple sources can be understood. This is not to say that dependency on one text excludes dependency on another but that if one text accounts for the data more effectively then it makes dependency on another text redundant.

CONCLUSION

In conclusion, it needs to be restated that the criteria are tests and not laws. They are not a fool-proof way of determining a case for literary

---

33. See Adam Winn's discussion on "Do Differences Matter?" in *Elijah-Elisha*, 33.
34. Conte, *Rhetoric of Imitation*, 28.

dependence. The lack of a standard and universal set of criteria means that it is up to the individual scholar to establish a set for his/her particular study. Some constants need to remain at the core of all criteria such as the historical plausibility of an argument and the meticulous analysis of shared elements such as vocabulary, theme, plot, and order. Also, the discussion of redundancy caused by other sources and the possibility of a common tradition and a general familiarity of a source text should be part of any set of criteria. Around this are certain flexible elements such as the status of the text and the discussion of differences. There will always be a certain amount of subjectivity to any case. No matter what the evidence for or against a case, different scholars will inevitably interpret data in multiple ways. Therefore, while the criteria are hugely beneficial in making sense of the relationship between texts, the limits of their application needs to be recognized. Finally, the criteria developed here largely represent a synthesis of many previously established criteria with certain new criteria aimed at making sense of the data collected. These criteria can be used for many texts and circumstances as there is a core base of criteria and some others which are flexible depending on the texts in question. These criteria can certainly be used in the attempt to explore the possibility of whether Mark used 1 Corinthians as a literary source.

— 3 —

Mark and Paul
A Brief History of Research

Throughout the history of Markan scholarship many scholars have noted similarities between the Gospel of Mark and the letters of Paul. These similarities have largely been theological. However, these similarities have only been noted as a by product of other arguments and few large-scale studies have been carried out to analyze these possible connections.

THE ANCIENT EVIDENCE

Nowhere in the Gospel of Mark does the author identify him or herself in any capacity. This is in line with many other biblical authors who do not identify themselves, in contradiction to the larger Hellenistic world of literature where it was common for an author to be identified.[1] Exactly when the name of Mark became attached to this gospel is not clear. A second century date is normally favored although late first century dates have been suggested.[2] Nevertheless, the gospel was likely to have been an anonymous document originally and in the first centuries of the church it became associated with Mark. Mark is one of the most common names in the Helle-

---

1. In general, the identity of a biblical author was not considered important. See Sternberg, *Poetics*, 33. Achtemeier, *Mark*, 125–26. See also Marcus, *Mark*, 1:17

2. Ibid. Hengel, *Studies*, 64–84, Anonymous Markan texts were still circulating in the fourth century. See Black, *Mark*, 151.

nistic world of the first century but only one Mark is known in early Church tradition and in the New Testament.[3]

The traditional view of the Gospel of Mark has been that the author was a follower and chronicler of the words of Peter. This view has largely developed from the fragment, preserved by Eusebius in the fourth century, known as the Papias testimony. Eusebius quotes a now lost text written by Papias, the Bishop of Hierapolis in Asia Minor, in the early second century.[4] Papias wrote that Mark was the interpreter of Peter and accurately wrote down everything Peter told him concerning Jesus. Papias adds that Mark did not omit or add anything. In spite of the text's apologetic tone it has dominated the discussion of Mark's sources for nearly two millennia. However, New Testament texts do not appear to make such a connection and, rather, connect Mark to Paul as do a handful of other ancient texts.

The New Testament

In the New Testament, Mark is a figure connected to Paul and is mentioned many times in Acts.[5] Mark or John Mark is a minor figure who appears to have had a tumultuous relationship with the apostle. In Acts 13:13 Mark abandons Paul while travelling to Perga and in 15:36–41 Paul shows some resentment towards Mark by refusing to allow Barnabas to bring Mark on their journey.[6]

Mark is also mentioned in the Pauline corpus in Col 4:10, Phil 1:24, and 2 Tim 4:11. The figure is generally portrayed positively, as opposed to the turbulent relationship seen in Acts, and is a valued follower of Paul.

A reference in 1 Peter also links Mark to Paul's circle (1 Pet 5:12–13) where Mark is mentioned as sending good greetings along with the apostle. However it is not clear if all these references are to the same person or whether or not this is reflective of any historical reality.

---

3. Marcus, *Mark*, 1:18.
4. Eusebius, *Hist. eccl.* III 39.15–16.
5. Acts 12:12, 25; 13:5, 13; 15:36–41.
6. Black, *Mark*, 25–49.

Hippolytus

The next reference to Mark and Paul together comes in the third century from the first anti-pope, Hippolytus of Rome.[7] However, Hippolytus does not link the two figures but rather lists them side by side. It may reflect some form of association between the two but this would be pure assumption and cannot be verified.[8]

"Adamantius" and the Apostolic Constitutions

Moving to the fourth century Mark is once again connected to Paul. In the text *De recta in Deum fide* (*The Dialogue on the Orthodox Faith*) Mark is identified as a co-worker of Paul's along with Luke. This text, often called "Adamantius" after one of the primary characters, probably originates in the early fourth century in Asia Minor or Syria.[9] It takes the form of a dialogue between the orthodox Adamantius and the heretic Megethius.

However, it should be noted that like the Papias testimony the language is apologetic and the author may be seeking to show Mark's authority by appealing to well recognized and authoritative texts.[10] Later in the fourth century and again from Syria, the *Apostolic Constitutions* link Mark and Luke to Paul but reduce their role to associates of Paul as opposed to apostles themselves.[11] However, the tradition that Mark was a follower of Peter persists throughout early Christianity. None of the ancient authorities connect Mark and Paul based on literary and theological terms but rather base their conclusions on church tradition and the brief references in the New Testament that connect the two. These references, therefore, have little use in terms of proposing a literary connection between Mark and Paul but serve to show how apologetic texts can dominate the interpretation of a text.

---

7. *Haer.* 7.30.1.
8. Black, *Mark,* 115–18. Lane, *Gospel of Mark,* 7–12.
9. Black, *Mark,* 149.
10. Ibid.
11. *Const. Ap.* 2.7.57. Black, *Mark,* 152–53.

The Quest for Mark's Sources

THE NINETEENTH CENTURY

F. C. Baur (1847)

Ferdinand Christian Baur (1792–1860) of the Tübingen School saw Mark as being a synthesis of Petrine and Pauline theology and used this to date Mark early in the second century C.E.[12] In Baur's view Luke was a thoroughly Pauline gospel while Matthew was Jewish in nature. Looking at Mark, Baur saw both Jewish and Gentile elements and concluded that Mark must be a synthesis of both Matthew and Luke and, therefore, representative of both Pauline and Petrine Christianity.[13]

Gustav Volkmar (1857 and 1870)

Gustav Volkmar, in opposition to the Tübingen School, raised the question of Mark's relationship to Paul in 1857. Volkmar, an early proponent of Markan priority, argued that the Gospel of Mark was representative of Pauline Christianity and was directed against Judeo-Christianity.[14] Following from this he argued that the composition of Mark, in the words of G. Stanton, ". . . evoked a Judaizing response, entitled the *Preaching of Peter*, a revised Mark plus the first half of Acts. Then canonical Luke-Acts was produced as a Paulinist reply and that in turn provoked a second Jewish-Christian reaction in the form of canonical Matthew."[15] Volkmar referred to Mark as being a ". . . paulinische Evangelium."[16] Essentially Volkmar's claim was that Mark's gospel was Pauline theology in narrative form. In 1870 Volkmar continued his theory and presented Mark as a pedagogical document thoroughly grounded in Pauline theology: "Inhalt der Erzählungen ist durchweg als sinnbildliche Darstellung paulinischer Lehre zu begreifen, so viel Überlieferungsstoff derein verwebt sein mag."[17] He goes on to describe Mark as ". . . einer der geistvollsten und einflußreichsten Schriftsteller, die es

---

12. Telford, *Theology*, 185. Kee, *Good News*, 2. Crossley, *Date*. 47. For an overview of Baur's career and contribution to Markan studies see, Kealy, *Hisotry*, 1:406–11.

13. Neil and Wright, *Interpretation*, 28. See also Fuller, "Baur Versus Hildenfeld," 357–358. For Baur's original argument see Baur, *Kritische*, 540–54.

14. Stanton, *Gospel*, 26. See also, Tuckett, "Griesbach Hypothesi," 34. Kealy, *History*, 457–58, 484–85.

15. Fuller, "Baur Versus Hildenfeld," 368–69.

16. Volkmar, *Die Religion Jesu*, xix, see also, 277–336.

17. Volkmar, *Die Evangelien*, 644.

nach Paulus gegeben hat."[18] It should be noted here that for Volkmar, Paul was not the only source for Mark but rather the gospel was a combination of Pauline theology, Old Testament, and traditional material.[19] Volkmar's argument has largely received a negative response throughout the history of scholarship and is often ignored altogether. Wrede provides a positive note and described Volkmar's 1870 commentary, which contained part of his argument of Mark's use of Paul, as ". . .the most perceptive and shrewd, and to my mind altogether the most important, that we possess on Mark."[20] However, Wrede is quick to point out the failings of Volkmar's work.

> The sum total of what is false and impossible in his work is great in things both great and small. Volkmar takes little account of tradition and has an exaggerated interest in the creative power of the "didactic poet."[21]

An interesting and aggressive attack on Volkmar came from Strauss who wrote in a letter in 1861:

> Einen närrischen Kauz, der aber nicht ohne einzelne lichte Blicke ist, habe ich in Volkmar, in seiner Religion Jesu, kennen gelernt; es ist Tollheit, was er vorbringt, doch nicht ohne Methode, und leider ist diese Methode zum Theil die Baur'sche: d. h. es fällt mir manchmal schwer, zwischen Baurs Vordersätzen und seinen Folgerungen den Graben zu ziehen der die Consequenzen abscnitte.[22]

This extract illustrates how poorly Volkmar's work was received. R. H. Fuller described Volkmar's work as ". . . *Tendenzkritik* run wild."[23] In fact, it is hard not to agree with Volkmar's critics as his claims do appear to be without method and direction.

---

18. Ibid., 647.

19. For a brief discussion of Volkmar's work in *Die Evangelien* see, Schmitals, "Zur Kritik der Formkritik," 275–313. See also, Wildemann, *Das Evangelium*. By far the most comprehensive overview of Volkmar's work is the posthumous essay by Anne Vig Skoven. Vig Skoven, "Mark," 13–27.

20. Wrede, *Messianic Secret*, 284.

21. Ibid.

22. This extract is provided in Schmitals, "Zur Kritik der Formkritik," 308–9.

23. Fuller, "Baur Versus Hildenfeld," 369.

The Quest for Mark's Sources

THE TWENTIETH CENTURY

M. Werner (1923)

The influential 1923 work by M. Werner argued that there is no connection between Mark and Paul beyond the level of coincidence.[24] Werner argued that although Mark, like Paul, was representative of Gentile Christianity it was separate and independent to Paul. Werner noted that many important Pauline themes were missing in Mark and concluded from this that whatever similarities there are were common to all early Christians or shared by the same strands of Christianity upon which both traditions were dependent.[25] Werner concluded that ". . . there cannot be the slightest idea of an influence of Pauline theology in the Gospel of Mark."[26] Werner's work was influential and seemed to close the door on any research into the connection between Mark and Paul. However, his work did not silence the idea completely.

B. W. Bacon (1925)

B. W. Bacon discusses Mark and Paul in his argument for the dating of Mark to C 75 C.E.[27] For Bacon, unlike Werner, Mark was the interpreter of Paul but was not dependent upon the letters themselves. The basic premise of Bacon's argument was the same as Volkmar's in that Mark was putting Pauline theology into narrative form.[28] One example of this comes in Mark 4:1–34 and the collection of parables found there. What draws attention is the theme of outsiders not being able to understand the parables and only a select few being able to comprehend what is actually being said.

> This apologetic is undoubtedly related to that of Paul in Rom. 9–11. For the purposes of developing it Mark utilises a logion about the "hiding of the mystery" which also plays a great part in

---

24. Werner, *Der Einfluss*.
25. Telford, *Theology*, 169.
26. Werner, *Der Einfluss*, 247. Translation provided by Telford, *Theology*, 168.
27. Bacon, *Gospel*.
28. See Baird, *History*, 2:301–2. Bacon also saw traditional Petrine material in the pages of Mark as well as Q. Essentially Mark harmonizes Petrine and Pauline theology in a manner similar to that envisioned by Baur.

the thought of Paul, though traceable in a form antecedent to both in the Wisdom literature.[29]

Another example Bacon gives is the abandonment of the food-laws in Mark 7:1–23 where Jesus ". . . swept away all distinction of meats and thereafter had extended his mission of mercy to gentiles also."[30] Paul, for Bacon, is behind these elements of Mark.[31] There is one part of Bacon's proposal that does argue for a direct literary dependence, namely the Last Supper/Eucharist in Mark 14:22–25 and 1 Cor 11:23–26. The level of literary connection and use of common phrases was for Bacon clear ". . . evidence for direct use."[32] For Bacon, "Paul is original. Mark is dependent."[33] Ultimately Bacon shies away from any claim of large scale literary dependence and concluded that it was not possible to prove dependence of Mark on Paul.[34]

W. Marxsen (1956)

Marxsen, using redaction criticism, argued that Mark cannot be compared to Paul in full but rather Mark's treatment of the various traditions which he inherited needs to be taken into account. He further argued that:

> Mark ties together two "strands" of primitive Christian preaching: The Pauline kerygma and the (so-called) synoptic tradition. In both strands we find the paradox inherent in the connection between the eschatological and the historical event, though with varying emphasis. Whereas Paul is basically content to assert the "that" of Jesus' humanity, the individual tradition here is more graphic. But even here we may not ignore what form history has demonstrated, viz., that this tradition is not concerned with the

---

29. Bacon, *Gospel*, 263.

30. Ibid. Crossley rejected this as being too vague and with little evidence for a Pauline influence. However, as Crossley places the composition of Mark in the late thirties or early forties in the first century C.E. the real issue is in which direction a possible influence would be. Crossley, *Date*, 48.

31. Bacon, *Gospel*, 264.

32. Ibid., 269.

33. Ibid.

34. Ibid. Another argument used by Bacon is the rejection of the Son of David Christology in both Mark and Paul in favor of a higher Son of God Christology. See Bacon, *Gospel*, 264. Crossley again rejects this as simply being too vague with no real points of specific connection. Crossley, *Date*, 51.

biographical but with the kerygmatic. Once again, therefore, Mark proves to be the consolidator.[35]

Marxsen goes on to say that Mark "...occupies a position between Paul and the anonymous tradition on the one hand, and the later evangelists on the other."[36] Marxsen's argument, while not proposing direct dependence, is important because it re-introduced the idea that there is a connection between the Gospel of Mark and the letters of Paul which had been absent from scholarship for some time. Through the use of redaction criticism, Marxsen identified possible points of connection that it was not possible for Werner to identify since Werner was writing before the advent of this methodology.

J. C. Fenton (1957)

J. C. Fenton explored the possible thematic connections between Mark and Paul.[37] Fenton's primary concern was to show that Mark was a Pauline gospel. This was done through the perspective that elements of Pauline theology can "...help to bring out the meaning of Mark."[38] Fenton explored many areas such as the theme of fulfilment which covers many areas such as time, scripture, law, temple, and Israel.[39] He also looked at the themes of hiding and revealing, defeat and victory, Jesus as Lord, faith and discipleship, and discussion of the future.[40]

Fenton's brief study is important in the history of the debate of Mark's possible connection to Paul because it introduced a thematic element of the debate. Previous work has mainly been carried out on the level of theology with some small work on the literary level. Fenton's work added a third dimension to the search for a connection.

Ralph Philip Martin (1978)

Ralph P. Martin saw Mark as being a gospel that was written in response to Pauline theology and the situations that arose because of it.[41] The situation

---

35. Marxsen, *Mark*, 216.
36. Ibid.
37. Fenton, "Mark and Paul," 89–112.
38. Ibid., 91–92.
39. Ibid., 92–97.
40. Ibid., 92–112.
41. Martin, "Theology," 23–26. For an overview of Martin's career and contribution to

in which Mark was composed ". . . arose after Paul's death or at least in areas where the influence of Paul's kerygmatic theology had sufficiently been diluted as to suggest a loss of grip on the historical events underlying his kerygma."[42] Martin's view of the Gospel of Mark is that the author is largely an historian as opposed to a biographer and sought to emphasize the humanity of Jesus and not his spirituality. Martin saw this emphasis on the spiritual Christ in the early Christian world as stemming from Paul but it had gone far from Paul's true meaning which revolved around the cross as did Mark's gospel.[43] Therefore, Martin saw Mark as attempting to bring people back to Paul's theology by placing ". . . the essence of Paul's thought. . ."[44] into a dramatization of Jesus' life, thus bringing Paul's theology back to the roots of Christianity. Mark is turning Pauline theology into narrative and expressing it in a way that Paul was not able to.[45]

Michael D. Goulder (1992)

Michael Goulder saw Mark as being a Pauline gospel along with the Gospel of John.[46] For Goulder, this was evident in the ambiguous portrayal of Jesus' family in Mark and Jesus' regular clashes with the Pharisees. Goulder argues that:

> . . . it would be a simple hypothesis to explain the anti-family tendency if Mark were a Pauline Christian embattled against the Jerusalem church's hegemony.[47]

His basic argument is that Mark was a Pauline gospel that was opposed to the Jerusalem centered early church and was more in line with the Pauline mission to the Gentiles, and that this is represented by the generally negative representation of the disciples and members of Jesus' family in the gospel. Added to this are Jesus' confrontations with the Pharisees throughout the

---

Markan scholarship see Kealy, *History,* 349–52.

    42. Martin, *Mark,* 161.

    43. Kealy, *History,* 351.

    44. Martin, *Mark,* 161.

    45. Ibid.

    46. Goulder, "Pauline in a Jacobite Church," 859–75.

    47. Ibid., 860. This idea has already been proposed, albeit in a much less worked out manner. See Crossan, "Mark," 97.

gospel, which Goulder sees as being representative of the Pauline conflicts with the Jerusalem church.

Goulder matched the eight confrontations that Jesus has with the Pharisees with elements of Paul, and concludes that these similarities are not accidents. From this Goulder infers that many of these episodes are the literary creation of the author of Mark.[48] The Pharisees in Mark are therefore an analogy for the Pharisaic Christians of the Jacobite church of the mid-first century who were the primary threat to the Pauline mission.[49]

However, although Goulder argues for Mark creating literature which is decidedly Pauline in nature, he proposes no form of literary dependence in any of the examples that he gives. For Goulder, the similarities are more general in nature reflecting a Pauline Christian author who was familiar with the central aspects of Pauline theology concerning the Law. This is then reflected throughout the gospel in the various confrontations that Jesus has with the Pharisees. Goulder, like Fenton before him, sees a Pauline influence in terms of theme and in Goulder's case this is very significant as he goes beyond the general nature of the influence and gives specific examples of influence while viewing Mark as a piece of constructed literature.

David Seeley (1993)

David Seeley, writing about rulership and service in Mark 10:41–45, describes certain parallels that reflect the theology of Paul, especially Rom 6:16–23.[50] The thrust of Seeley's article is that the ideas of rule and service find no precedence together in the Hebrew Bible or in apocryphal and pseudepigraphal texts. In Mark 10:45 Jesus predicts his death and says that the Son of Man is a servant and that his life is given for many. Seeley finds precedence for this in Rom 6:16–23 which is the only other early Christian text which speaks of a death as liberation from slavery and service. While acknowledging that this theory had been proposed before and largely rejected, Seeley believes it needs to be reconsidered for more reasons beyond the fact that it is found in both texts.[51] Another reason for this theory's reappraisal is Mark's treatment of sources. If Mark was a collector of tradi-

48. Goulder, "Pauline in a Jacobite Church," 873.
49. Ibid., 874.
50. Seeley, "Rulership and Service," 234–50.
51. Seeley, "Rulership and Service," 247. This theory has been proposed by both Bacon and Taylor. Bacon, *Gospel*, 242–271. Taylor, *Gospel*, 445–46.

tions and familiar with them, as many view him, then surely he would have been familiar with Paul who was a prominent figure in the early Christian world.[52] Also, Seeley sees it as highly unlikely that three of Paul's most important themes, the Eucharist, baptism, and Jesus' death, would appear in Mark 10:38–39, 45 with no intended allusion.[53] Lastly ". . . the author of the Second Gospel should be thought of as a creative intellect, capable of appropriating another's ideas in a less than explicit manner if suited to his purpose."[54]

This latter claim is significant in that it proposes that the author of Mark was quite capable of being creative in his treatment of sources, and that allusions to sources could be subtle in nature. However, Seeley views the absence of certain Pauline themes as being evidence that the author of Mark was not entirely in line with Pauline thinking. "Mark is indirectly acknowledging a theologian he could not completely ignore, but whose theology he did not fully approve of."[55]

William R. Telford (1999)

Telford initially drew comparisons between Mark and Paul in 1995 and had the following to say:

> . . . it may be significant that Mark's Gospel and the Pauline Epistles are the earliest extant writings of early Christianity that we possess, that both writers evince a similar attitude to the Jewish law . . . that both present evidence of tension with the leaders of the Jerusalem church . . . and that both demonstrate a concern for Gentiles . . . a sensitivity to issues of table fellowship . . . and a regard for Eucharistic symbolism.[56]

Telford also noted some basic ideological similarities but this is as far as the discussion went and no analysis was offered. It was not until 1999 that Telford offered a more detailed look at Mark and Paul.

While making clear that he believed a connection to be there, Telford made note of several similarities between Mark and Paul. Both Mark and Paul discuss how to deal with the Roman state (Mark 12:13–17, Rom

---

52. Ibid.
53. Ibid.
54. Seeley, "Rulership and Service," 248.
55. Ibid., 249.
56. Telford, *Mark*, 124–25.

13:1–7). Both have a negative view of the Jerusalem-centered church.[57] Both have similar views of food laws, particularly the shared meal. Both share common terminology and favor the title ὁ υἱός τοῦ θεοῦ for Jesus as well as κύριος.[58] Other shared vocabulary includes λόγος and μυστήριον. There is a shared motif of a hardening of heart (Mark 3:5, 6:53, 8:17 and Rom 11:7, 2 Cor 3:14). There is a common catalogue of vices (Mark 7:21–3 and Rom 1:29–31).[59] Both also focus on the salvific nature of Jesus' death.[60]

Although Telford sees a connection he allows for the possibility of pre-Markan traditions being involved in some way and acknowledges that there are also many differences between Mark and Paul. However, he states that:

> With the development, moreover, of narrative-critical tools and an increasing sensitivity on the part of scholars to the nuances of narrative theology, Volkmar's original suggestion that Mark's Gospel is an allegorical presentation of Pauline teaching in the form of a narrative may be due, therefore, for a comeback.[61]

Telford offers a general overview of the many similarities noted between Mark and Pauline literature. He does not go into detail about the nature and strength of these similarities but does propose that further investigation is needed into the issue.

THE TWENTY-FIRST CENTURY

Joel Marcus (2000)

In an article in 2000 about Mark's relationship to Paul, Joel Marcus writes:

> Claiming that Mark is a Paulinist does not require that he agree with Paul about everything, and plausible reasons can be advanced for a later Paulinist wanting to write the story of the earthly Jesus. Martin Werner's assertion that the agreements between Mark and Paul reflect general early Christian viewpoints is not valued with regard to the theology of the cross, which was a controversial Pauline emphasis and a stress that the later Gospels attenuated

---

57. Telford, *Theology*, 164–65.
58. Ibid., 166–67.
59. Ibid., 168.
60. Ibid.
61. Ibid., 169.

Mark and Paul

in editing Mark. Contrary to Werner, Mark and Paul agree in ascribing Jesus' death to a combination of human and demonic opponents.[62]

For Marcus, it is not important that every aspect of Pauline theology appears in the Gospel of Mark for there to be a connection. Rather, strands of Pauline theology can be found and traced within the gospel's pages. Marcus asserts that the time has come for the question of Mark's relationship to Paul to be revisited.[63] Marcus places emphasis on the influence of Werner's work which has caused scholars who have noted similarities between Mark and Paul to be ". . . reluctant to posit a direct connection."[64] Marcus then explores, in this article, the cross-centered theology of both Mark and Paul and after noting similarities concludes:

> If these are coincidences, they are amazing coincidences. If not—and I think not—they provide further evidence of Pauline influence on Mark.[65]

Marcus again makes note of the similar cross-centered theology in his commentary on Mark 1–8 in the same year. Marcus identifies roughly eight areas in which Mark and Pauline literature are similar. These are as follows:

1. Both describe Jesus' message as εὐαγγέλιον.
2. Jesus' crucifixion is central to their theology.
3. Both emphasise victory over demonic powers.
4. Both see Jesus as the fulfilment of the Old Testament scriptures.
5. Both emphasise faith in Jesus as important.
6. Both have a negative view towards Peter and members of Jesus' family.
7. Both say that Jesus came to the sinners.
8. Both emphasise that Jesus came not only to the Jews but also to the Gentiles.[66]

Marcus seems convinced of a connection although the level and type of connection is not explored as this is not his primary concern. What is significant is that Marcus recognises that not everything needs to match. That

62. Marcus, "Mark," 473.
63. Ibid.
64. Ibid., 474.
65. Ibid., 487.
66. Marcus, *Mark*, 1:74.

Mark lacks certain Pauline themes and theology does not mean that there is no form of dependency. As Seeley had argued before Marcus, Mark was quite capable of using sources to his own purposes and may not have approved of all of Paul's teachings.

RECENT RE-INTEREST IN MARK AND PAUL

While Telford stated that the question of Mark's relationship to Paul was due for a comeback, and Marcus furthered this notion, it would take over ten years for this to begin to happen. Three recent publications have seen a shift in the scholarly treatment of the Gospel of Mark's relationship to the letters of Paul. The question, it appears, is firmly back on the table and it is no longer met with the scepticism it once was.

James G. Crossley and Michael F. Bird (2011)[67]

The volume of collected essays, *Paul and the Gospels,* does not focus solely on Mark and Paul but looks at Paul's relationship to the four canonical gospels and the Gospel of Thomas.[68] Two chapters are given over to Mark and Paul specifically. The first, by James G. Crossley, looks at the overlap between the two writers on matters such as the suffering and death of Jesus, the Gentile mission, the Law and Christology. Crossley concludes that these similarities can be ascribed to the general cultural context in which they were both writing. However, Crossley's extremely early dating of Mark means, for Crossley, that influence could go in either direction.

Michael F. Bird's contribution, "Mark: Interpreter of Peter and Disciple of Paul," looks at the dual influence on Mark of both Peter and Paul in a hypothesis reminiscent of F. C. Baur. Bird argues that Paul's influence only makes sense in the presence of Petrine traditions. While any new discussion is welcome, especially when it brings it to a wider audience, neither essay advances on previous engagement with the subject.

---

67. See my own review of this volume, Nelligan, Review of *Paul and the Gospels.*
68. Bird and Willits, *Paul and the Gospels.*

Mark and Paul

Tom Dykstra (2012)

Tom Dykstra's *Mark, Canonizer of Paul* represents a significant shift in the ongoing discussion of Mark's relationship to Paul as it is the first modern monograph exclusively dedicated to the subject.[69] Dykstra views as highly flawed the older models of Mark which view the gospel writer as a collector of various written and oral traditions. He carefully creates a model based around intertextuality and imitation, with Greco-Roman literary models being at its base. Dykstra gives an in-depth analysis of the major Pauline themes found within Mark. He focuses on Mark and Paul's common defense of the Gentiles, the emphasis on the crucifixion, and the aggression shown towards members of Jesus' family. Dykstra also tackles literary issues by looking at a possible allusion to Colossians in the Parable of the Sower. A chapter is also devoted to Mark's appropriation of Pauline language, something which both Telford and Marcus have indicated before. Dykstra also argues that Jesus' life, as presented by Mark, is modelled after Paul's. He concludes that ". . . one of Mark's literary goals was to validate Paul as the premier apostle and consequently Paul's epistles as the scripture in which the true gospel can be found."[70]

Dykstra's work is significant because it shifts the discussion into the literary realm and away from purely historical and theological concerns. It also shifts Mark and Paul's literary construction in the sphere of Greco-Roman imitation.

The de Gruyter Volumes (2014)

This two-volume work represents the collected work of over two-dozen scholars on the issue of Mark's relationship to Paul.[71] It is, by far, the largest collected work on the issue carried out to date. The first volume contains essays dealing with Mark and Paul in their own context. It is, however, the second volume that concerns us here. It is in this volume that arguments for and against Pauline influence on Mark are outlined. Volkmar's original position is clearly explained by Anne Vig Skoven[72] while Joel Marcus' paper

---

69. Dykstra, *Mark*.
70. Ibid., 241–42.
71. Wischmeyer et al., *Paul and Mark*. Becker et al., *Mark and Paul*.
72. Vig Skoven, "Mark," 13–27.

The Quest for Mark's Sources

"Mark—Interpreter of Paul" is reprinted and updated.[73] Heike Omerzu provides a critical outline of the history of research[74] while Eve-Marie Becker looks at the literary activity behind Paul and Mark.[75]

Four papers are given over to comparing texts while four look at shared topics and perspectives. Oda Wischmeyer compares Rom 1:1–7 and Mark 1:1–3 and also revisits the role of εὐαγγέλιον which has previously been explored by Marxsen.[76] Jan Dochhorn argues against Pauline influence on Mark in a view more along the lines of traditional pre-Markan tradition theories.[77] Other essays sit on the fence while some argue both for and against Pauline influence. There is simply not the space here to go through the ins and outs of every argument as there are over thirty-five papers contained in the two volumes. However, they show that a healthy debate is rapidly growing around the topic in scholarship. From works like this others will follow leading to more thorough and in-depth research.

CONCLUSION

The above reveals that the question of Mark and Paul has never been fully explored nor has it disappeared. Some have proposed connections and some have tried to dismiss them. Some scholars have been more vehement than others in proposing connections and some have seen the slightest of connections while others see more in-depth parallels. The similarities noted fall into some basic categories: theme, theology and vocabulary. There is naturally a certain amount of overlap between these categories. Vocabulary links can be indicators of shared themes and aspects of theology while a certain theme can be tied to shared theological elements.

What becomes apparent from this secondary literature is that the argument has almost come full circle, beginning with Baur and Volkmar in the nineteenth century and re-emerging recently with Dykstra and others; the issue is firmly back on the table. It should be explored in more detail and warrants a more in-depth literary study.

---

73. Marcus, "Mark," 29–49.
74. Omerzu, "Paul and Mark," 51–61.
75. Becker, "Earliest Christian *Literary Activity*," 87–105.
76. Wischmeyer, "Romans 1:1–7 and Mark 1:1–3," 121–46.
77. Dochhorn, "Man and the Son of Man," 147–68.

—4—

First Corinthians and Mark
An Overview

From Volkmar to Dykstra many commentators have speculated as to the nature of the relationship between Paul and Mark. Some have proposed that any similarities are pure coincidence, while others have proposed more direct literary influence. One thing is for certain, there is no consensus. How, then, does one begin to tackle such a topic, the study of which has lacked clear direction within scholarship? Certainly, ploughing through the entire Pauline corpus and comparing it to Mark is a thoroughly daunting task and one that is too broad to yield any manageable results. Therefore, a single Pauline letter would be an appropriate place to begin. The advantage of focussing on a single letter to compare to Mark is that it allows for more detailed analysis which can get to the core of each text without being spread too thin. Which Pauline letter, then, should be compared to Mark?

The letter chosen should be an undisputed letter. While later Pauline epistles may offer points for discussion, the arguments would, however, be undermined by questions over the text's authenticity. First Thessalonians is generally held to be the earliest extant Pauline letter and is dated to around 50 C.E. and may have been sent from Corinth.[1] First Corinthians and Galatians are generally held to have been the next letters written, possibly at the

---

1. Betz, "Paul," 191. Krentz, "First and Second Epistles to the Thessalonians," 515.

same time, around 52–55 C.E.[2] One of these three early letters may be an appropriate place to begin as they are considered to be authentic and present a wealth of material to compare to Mark. The letter to the Romans also presents this possibility. Which of these letters, then, should be chosen?

First Corinthians offers some interesting possibilities for investigation. Both contain shared themes such as food and the way in which followers of Jesus should act. Both texts also narrate the inauguration of the Eucharist. Therefore, 1 Corinthians may prove an appropriate text to investigate. However, before beginning a large scale investigation, it is necessary to look at the nature of both texts as this will ultimately affect how the texts are approached.

GENRE

When dealing with two starkly different texts such as 1 Corinthians and Mark, the question of genre naturally arises. How should genre be approached and how does it change how this investigation will proceed? While First Corinthians can be easily placed into the category of Hellenistic letter writing, Mark's Gospel can be somewhat more difficult to categorize. While the present investigation of Mark's possible use of 1 Corinthians does not hinge on Mark's genre, it is certainly worth considering as a text's genre can hugely influence how a text is interpreted. "Generic expectations of works are often the single most important guide to their interpretations—what readers conceive the genre of a text to be—newspaper article, poem, detective story, telephone book—determined how they read it, what they expect to find, and what they learn from it."[3]

Genre can be understood as a code of communication shared by certain texts with broad stylistic similarities. For example, the epic poetry of Homer, Apollonius Rhodius, and Virgil all share conventions for plot, characterization, and speech, among other aspects. These conventions are different from tragedy which uses its own distinct conventions. Therefore, we can expect differing things from different genres. The uncertainty of Mark's genre makes it difficult to know what to expect from the text and how to interpret it.

Although a plethora of suggestions have been made for Mark, two theories stand out as the most plausible. The first is that the Gospel of

---

2. Betz, "Paul," 191.
3. Tolbert, *Sowing the Gospel*, 48.

Mark is an historical narrative in the same vein as Old Testament texts. The second is that Mark is a Hellenistic *bioi*. However, neither possibility fully satisfies. Therefore, for the sake of argument Mark can be considered part of an emerging "gospel" genre, unique to early Christianity.

Genres can be used as an unhelpful term forcing the texts into categories, boxing them off from other texts. However, it does not need to be unhelpful or an obstacle to overcome. The question of genre is not simple and it would be wise not to ignore it. Genres are not simple categories and static. Rather, they are fluid and ever changing with each new text that is written.[4] Just as members of a family may resemble one another, so can texts resemble other members of their particular genre; at the same time a family, like a genre, is made up of individual members. The emerging gospel genre is testament to this fluidity and the question of genre can further help scholars to understand these unique modes of communication.

It is not just readers that consider genre, they are also a consideration for the author. The genre is what can make the writer understood.[5] This is likely to be part of the reason for the significant confusion over the genre of the gospels as they do not conform to any previous code of communication. They are something new. Their lack of conforming nature to existing genres does not, however, make them immune to existing methods of literary borrowing. Therefore, they should not be treated as such.

Some scholars consider discussion of genre to be illegitimate.[6] However, such an approach would be unwise and ignores the reality that ancient authors, rhetoricians, and commentators were keenly aware of genre and a text's place within the generic tradition. P. A. Miller describes genre as follows:

> Genres can now be seen as variable, linguistic responses to the changing conditions of communal life, which derive their evolutionary and recombinatory possibilities from the set of accepted patterns of usage available to a given socio-cultural grouping at a particular time. Consequently, there can be no question of doing violence to a work by reading it in light of its generic background, because that background constitutes the very linguistic and material base which makes the work itself possible.[7]

---

4. Conte, *Genres*, 127.
5. Ibid., 114.
6. See Miller, *Lyric Texts*, 37.
7. Ibid., 44.

Such an approach to genre is adopted here. This approach allows genre to be recognized and be part of the discussion but does not allow genre to become a restrictive tool, hampering any analysis of the texts. As ancient texts freely borrowed from texts in other genres, genre provides no problems when considering the question of whether the author of Mark knew and used 1 Corinthians.

STYLE

The Gospel of Mark is significantly longer than 1 Corinthians and the styles of the two texts are also markedly different, largely resulting from their differing genres. Paul is constructing detailed theological arguments in response to the needs of the Corinthian community while the author of Mark is constructing a narrative story centered around the life of Jesus. Paul spends considerable length constructing arguments while Mark's narrative moves along at lightning speed. The episodic nature of Mark's texts can see important scenes, such as the Temptation, play out in just two verses. The episodic nature of Mark finds a parallel in the Old Testament primary history (Genesis—2 Kings).[8] This can be seen throughout the following chapters where Mark continuously relies on Genesis—2 Kings as a literary source. Winn has skilfully shown that the style of Mark, with its miracle and prophet motifs, shares more in style with the Elijah-Elisha narrative than any other extant text.[9] While the genre may be something new and the literary techniques akin to those used in the Greco-Roman world, the style is close to that already established by the author of the Elijah-Elisha narrative.

BROAD SIMILARITIES

The first step is to look at the broad similarities within the two texts. These would likely be theological or thematic in nature. For example, early on in both texts baptism becomes an important theme. Both 1 Cor 5 and Mark 6:14–29 deal with a man living with someone prohibited by Jewish law. The central portions of each text also contain lengthy segments dealing with

---

8. Winn, *Elijah-Elisha*, 66.
9. Ibid., 61–68.

food. Both touch on marriage and divorce and finally, both narrate the inauguration of the Eucharist. These would be good places to begin.

Taking the similarities noted above the potential for investigation looks as follows:

First Corinthians	Mark[A]
1:14–17—Baptism	1:4–8—Baptism
5:1–13—Man living with his father's wife	6:14–29—Man living with his brother's wife
7:1–16—Marriage and divorce	10:1–12 Marriage and divorce
8:1–13—Idol food	6:30–44—Feeding the five thousand
10:14–11:1—Return to idol food	8:1–9—Feeding the four thousand
11:23–26—The Eucharist	14:22–25—The Eucharist

A. The order of Mark has been altered here to show the similarities with 1 Corinthians.

While it may be possible to further map out how 1 Corinthians may relate to Mark, the above table represents a good starting point on the back of which future research could begin. The point of departure for beginning such an investigation is naturally the start of each text. Therefore, the two sections about baptism should be probed. However, baptism is such a key component of most New Testament texts that the investigation should be extended to the surrounding sections in order to determine whether or not these texts are interrelated. Therefore, 1 Cor 1–2 will be compared to Mark 1:1–28 as this should provide a larger context for the discussion.

First Corinthians 5 and Mark 6:14–29 represent an area with a very close subject matter. The same can be said of 1 Cor 11:23–26 and Mark 14:22–25. However, the possibility of a literary connection between the two Eucharist accounts has often been rejected in favor of a common liturgical source. Therefore, extending the search to the sections surrounding the Eucharist accounts will help to determine whether or not they are connected.

While the discussion of marriage, divorce, and food could be fruitful, limiting the initial investigations to three points of interest would allow for a more in-depth discussion. Therefore, the three areas which will be compared an analyzed will be:

- 1 Cor 1–2 and Mark 1:1–28
- 1 Cor 5 and Mark 6:14–29
- 1 Cor 11:2–34 and Mark 14:1–25

The Quest for Mark's Sources

In doing this a consistent method of procedure is required throughout. A brief introductory analysis, which will outline the broad similarities between each text being investigated, will precede a detailed analysis. The detailed analysis will first look at the established parallels the Markan gospel has to other texts. These are mainly Old Testament texts but texts from the classical world will also be considered. Following this, the relevant sections of Mark and 1 Corinthians will be compared under the headings of context, theme, action/plot, order, completeness, and vocabulary. Then it will be necessary to compile the collected data and analyze it through the criteria for judging literary dependence, after which conclusions can be made. A case for literary dependence will only be made if the data indicates that this is a likely possibility.

—5—

Comparison and Analysis of 1 Corinthians 1–2 and Mark 1:1–28

INTRODUCTORY ANALYSIS

First Corinthians 1–2 and Mark 1:1–28 have been chosen because of their respective positions within their larger literary contexts. They are the opening sections of the texts and if they are connected then this is an appropriate place to begin the investigation. They also contain baptism as a key theme. First Corinthians 1–2 forms part of a larger unit which runs to the end of chapter 4.[1] However, four chapters is a large body of text to analyze as an initial area and would not allow time or space to explore other parts of the letter and gospel. Therefore the investigation will be limited to the first half of this unit of text.

The reasons for only looking at Mark 1:1–28 is partly because this is where parallels with 1 Cor 1–2 were found. Mark 1:1–28 can be divided into seven sections and each section corresponds in some way with a part of 1 Cor 1–2 which can be divided into eight sections, which are as follows:

1. Epistolary prescript (1 Cor 1:1–3)
2. Thanksgiving (1 Cor 1:4–9)
3. Divisions in the Corinthian church (1 Cor 1:10–13)

---

1. Most commentators treat chapters 1–4 as a larger unit within the letter as a whole. See Conzelmann, *1 Corinthians*, 19–93. Hays, *First Corinthians*, 21–79. Fitzmyer, *First Corinthians*, 136–227.

4. Paul recalls baptizing (1 Cor 1:14–17)

5. The power and wisdom of God (1 Cor 1:18–25)

6. The call of those in Corinth (1 Cor 1:26–31)

7. Proclaiming Christ crucified (1 Cor 2:1–5)

8. True wisdom and understanding (1 Cor 2:6–16)

In Mark 1:1–28 there are seven sections which are as follows:

1. Introduction (Mark 1:1–3)

2. The appearance of John the Baptist (Mark 1:4–8)

3. The baptism of Jesus (Mark 1:9–11)

4. Jesus in the wilderness (Mark 1:12–13)

5. Jesus goes to Galilee (Mark 1:14–15)

6. Jesus calls four disciples (Mark 1:16–20)

7. Jesus performs an exorcism (Mark 1:21–28)

The sections listed above for 1 Cor 1–2 are largely standard and found within the many commentaries on the letter. They also, in general, follow the UBS and Nestle-Aland editions of the Greek New Testament.[2] While most divisions are the same, some do not follow the traditional divisions and warrant further discussion. Unusually, 1 Cor 1:10–17 has been split into two smaller units of text, namely 1 Cor 1:10–13 and 1 Cor 1:14–17. Most texts and commentators do not do this and opt to keep 1 Cor 1:10–17 as one unit of text.[3] There is, however, an internal division. Although 1 Cor 1:14–17 is much shorter than 1 Cor 1:10–13 it is these first four verses that receive the bulk of the scholarly attention because they provide a glimpse into the situation in Corinth. Thus, when Paul shifts his focus somewhat in v. 14, it is barely noted.[4] There is also some vocabulary that indicates that v. 14 is the beginning of a new section.

---

2. Both the UBS and Nestle-Aland editions divide the text with headings and paragraphs as follows: (1) 1 Cor 1:1–3. (2) 1 Cor 1:4–9.(3) 1 Cor 1:10–17. (4) 1 Cor 1:18–25. (5) 1 Cor 1:26–31. (6) 1 Cor 2:1–5. (7) 1 Cor 2:6–16.

3. See Conzelman, *1 Corinthians*, 30–39. Fitzmyer, *First Corinthians*, 136–51. Hays, *First Corinthians*, 21–24. Collins, *First Corinthians*, 67–86.

4. Conzelmann, Barrett, Collins and Fitzmyer all spend ample time analyzing vv 10–13 while vv14–17 receives much less attention. See Conzelmann, *1 Corinthians*, 30–39. Barrett, *First Epistle*, 40–49. Fitzmyer, *First Corinthians*, 136–51. Collins, *First Corinthians*, 67–86.

Comparison and Analysis of 1 Corinthians 1–2 and Mark 1:1–28

The opening words of this section, εὐχαριστῶ [τῷ θεῷ] (1:14), are the same as the opening of the second section (1 Cor 1:4–9). Therefore, a division has been made here. One commentary recognizes the internal divisions within 1 Cor 1:10–17. W. F. Orr and J. A. Walther hold 1 Cor 1:10–17 together as a single unit of text but also sub-divides it into three smaller sections, namely vv. 10–13, vv. 14–16, and v. 17.[5] Orr and Walther recognize the shifts within this section between Paul's discussion of the growing factionalism in Corinth and his discussion of his own baptizing activity in that city. They, interestingly, separate v17 from the rest of the section because Paul begins to discuss his apostolic mission of spreading the good news, which changes the subject yet again. However, baptism is still a theme in v. 17. Rather, Paul introduces a new theme here alongside baptism, namely the power of the cross, which will be the driving theme of the next section, 1 Cor 1:18–25. First Corinthians 1:17 acts more as a transitional verse between the two sections instead of acting as its own unit. It connects the theme of baptism to the power of the cross. Therefore, v. 17 will be kept together with vv. 14–16 and treated as one unit. One final consideration in splitting 1 Cor 1:10–17 into two smaller units is that the similarities with Mark are in two different sections.

A few points about 1 Cor 2 also need to be mentioned. Most commentators divide this chapter at v. 6 resulting in two sections, 1 Cor 2:1–5 and 1 Cor 2:6–16.[6] There is a shift in theme in this chapter which is why it is split. In 2:1–5 Paul discusses proclaiming Christ crucified while in 2:6–16 Paul talks about the true wisdom of God. The two are, however, linked as Paul presents the cross as being the true wisdom of God. The two are also linked by the word πνεῦμα, which is central to the chapter.[7] Because of this, 1 Cor 2 will be kept together as one single unit in the detailed analysis. Although it will be treated as one unit of text it is recognized that there is a division in this section. This is also determined, somewhat, by how Mark appears to be using the text.

Dividing Mark is a somewhat easier task as Mark writes in short episodes making division in the text relatively simple. The UBS Greek New Testament divides Mark 1:1–28 into six sections and includes 1:1–3 as part of John the Baptist's preaching forming the larger section of 1:1–8. The

---

5. Orr and Walther, *1 Corinthians*, 147–51.

6. Conzelmann, *1 Corinthians*, 53–69. Hays, *First Corinthians*, 61–79. Collins, *First Corinthians*, 115–38. Barrett, *First Epistle*, 35–46.

7. Fitzmyer, *First Corinthians*, 169.

The Quest for Mark's Sources

Nestle-Aland edition does likewise. However, there is a shift within this section (1:1–8) from the incipit and quote 1:1–3 to the narrative which begins with the appearance of John the Baptist in v. 4 therefore, 1:1–3 and 1:4–8 will be treated as separate sections.

The first few episodes in Mark, which make up 1:1–13, form an extended introduction to the gospel.[8] Some commentators treat 1:1–8 as an introduction and do not carry on to v.13.[9] Although 1:1–8 or 1:1–13 may be considered an introduction, these verses do contain subdivisions and these smaller blocks will be used here which will allow for analysis of the text in more detail. Marcus, in his commentary on Mark, includes 1:1–15 as part of a larger section, namely 1:1–28 and divides this into seven sections. The divisions used here are the same as those of Marcus.[10]

Why stop at 1:28? The narrative moves on and the chapter does not end here. Rather, 1:29 is the beginning of a new narrative flow as indicated by texts and commentaries.[11] In typical Markan fashion 1:29 begins with καὶ indicating the beginning of a new episode or anecdote. Therefore, it makes sense to divide the text here and to stop at this point as 1:29 marks the start of a series of healings which runs on until 2:12.

On the surface, it appears as if these two texts (1 Cor 1–2 and Mark 1:1–28) have absolutely nothing in common. They seem to deal with very different subject matters. First Corinthians 1–2 addresses very specific problems in a particular place. Yet Paul's responses and solutions to these problems could be applicable to people across the entire early Christian world who may have been facing similar problems. Therefore, if Mark were to incorporate elements of 1 Corinthians into his gospel it would have certain pastoral and pedagogical applications.

Nevertheless, the texts are different and Paul is writing a theological letter while Mark is writing a narrative gospel. So the two texts do indeed appear to be poles apart. However, in probing deeper certain similarities begin to appear such as the themes of baptism and the spiritual call which permeate both texts. Following a trial-and-error comparison of these texts a series of connections appears. The working hypothesis will be that each of the sections of Mark is based, partly, on the various sections in 1

---

8. Hooker, *Gospel*, 31–66.
9. Lane, *Gospel of Mark*, 39–76.
10. Marcus, *Mark*, 1:131–94.
11. The UBS and Nestle-Aland editions of the Greek New Testament begin a new section here. See Marcus, *Mark*, 1:195. Collins, *Mark*, 174. Hooker, *Gospel*, 70.

Comparison and Analysis of 1 Corinthians 1–2 and Mark 1:1–28

Corinthians. The following table highlights the aspect of each section that may correspond to another section.

First Corinthians 1–2	Mark 1:1–28[A]
Prescript—appeal to a higher power (1:1–3)	Incipit, prophecy and appeal to a higher power (1:1–3)
Thanksgiving—revelation (1:4–9)	Jesus' baptism—a revelation (1:9–11)
Brothers in Corinth. Fourfold division (1:10–13)	Brothers. Fourfold unity (1:16–20)
Paul recalls baptizing (1:14–17)	John baptizes (1:4–8)
Power/wisdom of God—delivering a message (1:18–25)	Jesus goes to Galilee—delivering a message (1:14–15)
Examining the call (1:26–31)	The Temptation—testing the call (1:12–13)
Demonstration of power, teaching, hiding, and revealing (2:1–16)	Synagogue—power, teaching, hiding, and revealing (1:21–28)

A. The order of the Markan text has been altered here in order to highlight the sections that correspond, in some way, to sections of 1 Corinthians. This is done purely as a matter of presentation.

DETAILED ANALYSIS

BEGINNINGS THAT BRING GOOD GREETING, GOOD NEWS (1 COR 1:1–3 AND MARK 1:1–3)

On the surface it would appear that these two openings are poles apart. Paul's opening section is an epistolary prescript in which he introduces himself along with Sosthenes and makes clear that he is speaking to the Corinthian church that he blesses with grace and peace. The letter is not only addressed to the Corinthian church but to every Christian.

On the other hand, Mark's gospel begins with the title-like sentence Ἀρχὴ τοῦ εὐαγγελίου Ἰησοῦ χριστοῦ [υἱοῦ θεοῦ] and moves into the conflated quote from Isaiah and Malachi which prophesises the sending of a messenger who will prepare the way of the Lord. This serves to introduce John the Baptist into the narrative and then Jesus.

59

The Quest for Mark's Sources

Initial General Comparison

Both texts recognize the authority of God and Jesus and both see authority and power as coming from God and not from earthly powers. In making observations it would be all too easy to dismiss Paul's beginning simply as a letter opening. It also serves to set the stage for Paul's argument to the Corinthians. In a similar fashion, Mark's opening verses should not be dismissed as mere introduction. Like 1 Cor 1:1–3 these verses set the stage for the following narrative.

Both share significant amounts of vocabulary. Many words that are found in 1 Cor 1:1–3 are found in Mark 1:1–3 such as ἀπόστολος (the verbal cognate ἀποστέλλω is found in Mark), Χριστός, Ἰησοῦς, θεός, κύριος, and αὐτός.

There are, however, obvious differences between the two texts that need to be recognized. Firstly, 1 Cor 1:1–3 contains no obvious scriptural quote. Paul is addressing his letter to a specific audience while Mark's audience remains unnamed. Similarly, Paul names himself while the author of Mark is left unidentified. Yet, despite these differences, there remain the similarities mentioned above such as the appeal to a higher power at the opening of both texts and the shared vocabulary. These will be discussed further below following a closer look at Mark's text and its sources.

Literary Aspects of Mark 1:1–3

Before being able to properly assess the similarities between 1 Cor 1:1–3 and Mark 1:1–3 some aspects of Mark need to be mentioned and discussed.

Parallels with Other Texts

In discussing other texts, classical texts will also be mentioned. This is done purely to show the many parallels to Mark. Dependency on classical texts is not assumed and cannot be explored in full here. Rather, classical texts are presented to show that Mark fits within the larger Greco-Roman literary world.

Comparison and Analysis of 1 Corinthians 1–2 and Mark 1:1–28

OLD TESTAMENT

Mark's reliance on the Old Testament can be seen quite clearly in these three opening verses with the conflated quote from Isaiah and Malachi. Considering that this quote forms the majority of these three verses they are, therefore, Mark's main sources at this point. Malachi, in particular, raises some interesting points. The quote comes from Mal 3:1. However, the notion of sending someone is repeated at the end of that same text, in connection with Elijah:

καὶ ἰδοὺ ἐγὼ ἀποστέλλω ὑμῖν Ηλιαν τὸν Θεσβίτην πρὶν ἐλθεῖν ἡμέραν κυρίου τὴν μεγάλην καὶ ἐπιφανῆ (Mal 3:22)

Following the partial quote in Mark, John the Baptist appears styled, quite clearly, after Elijah. Malachi could be the source of this and, therefore, plays an important role in the opening verses of Mark, extending beyond Mark 1:1–3.[12] The quote in Mark 1:1–3 becomes a form of a literary signpost leading the reader to make connections.

The use of ἀρχὴ is also interesting here. The use of ἀρχὴ with the absence of an article creates a title-like sentence which is reminiscent of some Old Testament and apocryphal texts such as Hosea, Proverbs and Song of Solomon (LXX).[13] The use of ἀρχὴ is also reminiscent of the opening, in the LXX, of Genesis which uses the noun along with the preposition ἐν. This has the effect of creating a feeling that this is something new, almost like a second creation.

NEW TESTAMENT

Parallels can also be found with Romans and Philippians. Rom 1:1 shares vocabulary with Mark such as Χριστός, Ἰησοῦς, εὐαγγέλιον, θεός, and ἀπόστολος, of which Mark uses the verbal cognate in v2. There is also a significant similarity with Philippians. The phrase Ἀρχὴ τοῦ εὐαγγελίου which appears in Mark 1:1 also appears in exactly the same form in Phil 4:15. These are the only two occurrences of this phrase in the entire New Testament and LXX.

While the opening of Romans and 1 Corinthians are similar, when compared to Mark, 1 Corinthians shares more vocabulary. First Corinthians

---

12. Marcus, *Mark*, 1:142.
13. Ibid., 1:141.

1:1–3 and Mark 1:1–3 share six words while Rom 1:1–3 only shares five common words. However, Romans shares a more striking similarity in that both share the word εὐαγγέλιον which is somewhat uncommon. The noun εὐαγγέλιον occurs seventy-six times in the New Testament and sixty occurrences of these are in Pauline letters. It is a word highly associated with the Pauline corpus. Therefore, Romans matches Mark more closely than 1 Corinthians in this instance. The shared words, apart from εὐαγγέλιον, are all common to the New Testament. Therefore, little to nothing can be said about dependence at this point. However, only Mark shares a cluster of words with Paul. It may reveal a general influence of Pauline letter writing on Mark.

Classical Texts

An interesting parallel to these opening verses of Mark can be found in a Roman inscription. Adam Winn, while discussing the Markan incipit, points out that the opening sentence of Mark's gospel is very like the Priene Inscription which was written in honour of the Emperor Augustus.[14] The similar portion reads as follows: ". . . since the birthday of the god, Augustus was the beginning of the good tidings . . ."[15] The similarities are striking to the opening of Mark. "Good tidings" in the Priene Inscription is represented by the noun εὐαγγελία the feminine form of εὐαγγέλιον, used in Mark.

Connections Between Mark 1:1–3 and Other Parts of 1 Cor 1–2

The phrase καθὼς γέγραπται appears in both texts. It appears in 1 Cor 1:21 and 2:9 and is used to introduce an Old Testament quotation as it is in Mark. It appears in Mark 1:2 (and again in 9:13 and 14:21). There are only a handful of uses of this introductory formula outside of the New Testament.[16] Within the New Testament, Mark and Luke-Acts use this phrase three times each while Matthew only uses it once. It does, however, appear in Paul some eighteen times with fourteen usages from Romans alone and two usages each in 1 and 2 Corinthians. It can be said, therefore, that this is a largely Pauline phrase. Mark's use of this phrase may indicate a general

---

14. Winn, *Purpose*, 97.
15. Ibid.
16. 2 Chr 25:4, 1 Esd 3:9, Tob 1:6, and Dan 9:13.

appropriation of Pauline language by Mark as indicated by Telford, Marcus, and Dykstra. Statistically, Paul is the likely source of this phrase. The verb γράφω is also used twice in 1 Cor 1–2 (1:19 and 1:31) without καθὼς. The noun εὐαγγέλιον occurs three times in this opening section of Mark and in 1 Cor 1:10–13 which uses its verbal form.

Detailed Comparison

Context

These are the opening verses of both texts and help to prepare the context for the narrative and arguments to come. In 1 Cor 1:1–3 Paul sets the scene by addressing the letter to a specific community and making clear from whom the letter is from. This is done along with a blessing which creates a generally friendly opening tone. In Mark 1:1–3 the author is also setting the scene by making clear who the text will be about and where that person came from. The effect of the quote is to show the cultural and religious background of the text and to show that John the Baptist is sent to prepare the way for Jesus. The tone is positive with the promise of making paths straight.

Theme

There are certain thematic similarities between these two opening sections which need to be discussed. These are the themes of freedom and higher powers. Conzelmann has noted that Paul's opening in v1, which states that his calling is by the θελήματος θεοῦ indicates a freedom.[17] This freedom is from other powers and commissioning bodies and in essence from earthly powers. The use of εὐαγγέλιον in Mark raises some issues connected with this freedom. Vespasian is an emperor highly associated with εὐαγγελία and Winn argues that this word was almost entirely associated with the emperor and, therefore, Mark's incipit is clearly a reference to this and is establishing Jesus as the true son of God and proclaiming a new world order—an alternative to the present Roman order.[18] Therefore, both Mark and Paul begin their texts with an appeal to a higher power, separate to and above earthly powers. The matters in Corinth that Paul discusses and the

---

17. Conzelmann, *1 Corinthians*, 20.
18. Ibid. Winn, *Purpose*, 92–99.

earthly story of Jesus, while the central aspects of their respective texts, are only one level of what is happening. Higher than the earthly matters is the authority of God to which both texts are appealing. While this is nothing significant in itself, as all biblical texts claim authority from God, when coupled with the shared vocabulary these two small sections become more alike that it outwardly appears. Appealing to God or a god in the opening of a text is normally found in classical literature (for example, the *Iliad*, *Odyssey*, and *Aeneid* all begin with appeals to gods or a muse) yet it is not always found in Jewish and Christian literature (Isa 1:2 is an example of when God is called upon early in a text). It is, however a consistent feature of Paul's letters and appears in every single one. This is not the case in the gospels; only Mark and John make God the focus of their opening verses. There is also some affinity between the theology of Paul in the opening of 1 Corinthians and the opening of Mark. Paul offers the Corinthians grace and peace from God. In Mark, through Isaiah, a messenger is sent to make paths straight and to prepare the way for the Lord. The affinity is found in the idea of God offering assistance in the form of grace and peace in Corinth and preparing the way in Mark. An immediate sense of God being present is in both texts and they are consistent with each other.

Both texts also appeal beyond their intended audience and to the whole world of Gentiles and both are possibly making reference to Malachi. Paul in 1 Cor 1:2 mentions ἐν παντὶ τόπῳ (in every place) while addressing the letter. The letter is, therefore, not addressed to only the Corinthians but to those who 'in every place' call on the name of Jesus. Ciampa and Rosner believe this to be a subtle reference to Mal 1:1 which says that Yahweh will come to be worshipped 'in every place' and, therefore, by Gentiles.[19] In Mark, the Malachi reference forms part of the prophecy of the arrival of both John the Baptist and Jesus who is τὸ εὐαγγέλιον τοῦ θεοῦ (v14). This good news is also for the Gentiles as revealed through the theme of insiders and outsiders in Mark. Therefore, both texts appeal beyond their audience to the whole world. References to Malachi are possibly at the root of this appeal in both texts, although it needs to be remembered that this possible reference to Malachi is not an overt one in 1 Corinthians.[20]

---

19. Ciampa and Rosner, *First Corinthians*, 57.

20. For example, the story of the Syrophoenician women is often seen as Jesus opening up the good news to the Gentiles. See Marcus, *Mark*, 1:461–71. The inclusiveness, in Mark, of the good news is further revealed by John the Baptist to whom all the countryside go. This appears to be foreshadowing this inclusiveness.

Comparison and Analysis of 1 Corinthians 1–2 and Mark 1:1–28

Action/Plot and Order

In terms of action/plot the differing genres make finding similarities in these areas unlikely. In terms of order, both open by indicating a higher power and then move onto a general message of good will for the recipient of the letter/gospel.

Vocabulary

There is some shared vocabulary at the start of both of these texts. The grouping of these shared words (ἀπόστολος and its verbal cognate, Χριστός, Ἰησοῦς, θεός, κύριος, and αὐτός) together in both texts is interesting, particularly when it is considered that Mark is the only gospel that shares these words with 1 Corinthians in the opening. The gospels do not have a standard opening as the epistles do and this suggests that Mark has been influenced by early Christian letter writing. Most of Paul's letters begin in a similar fashion as do the other letters in the New Testament. When this is considered it seems difficult to ignore the similarity of Mark's opening verses with that of the epistles. While these words are common, it is their placement in both texts that is significant. The fact that Mark's opening is similar to one used many times in Paul's letters and not in the other gospels is a significant piece of information as it makes it statistically more likely that Mark is using Paul's letters as a literary source.

Completeness

Many of the elements of 1 Cor 1:1–3 are matched, in some way, to Mark 1:1–3, although in a very general nature at this point.

Assessment and Conclusion

These sections show some similarities. A general similarity in terms of purpose has been seen in that both identify the presence of God and recognize Jesus as God's son. Both texts then move on to indicate good will. There is completeness and order to this, as well as some shared, albeit common, vocabulary. Mark shares this opening similarity with many of the Pauline epistles and is alone amongst the gospels in this style of opening. Therefore, there are grounds to suggest that Mark is connected to the letter writing tradition.

When these connections are noted, along with the connections to Romans, Philippians, the Priene Inscription, and the various other epistles in the New Testament a question begins to emerge; is Mark weaving texts together? That this type of weaving was common in the ancient world and particularly in Greek and Latin literature is illustrated by Damien Nelis who says that "The subtle interweaving of models in highly sophisticated patterns of imitation is pervasive in Latin poetry . . ." Nelis goes on to say that this interweaving follows from Greek literature.[21] If this is what Mark was doing it was nothing unusual and was actually common and expected in the Greco-Roman world. For example, in Theocritus' prologue, and indeed throughout his text, both Homer and Apollonius are imitated and used as models. It has been argued that by having a high level of intertextuality at the opening of the text, Theocritus is giving a signpost to the reader of the composition to follow. It indicates what is to be expected and what is to come.[22] Similarly in Mark 1:1–3 the reader is shown what to expect in the gospel. Ancient readers with knowledge of Old Testament texts would undoubtedly notice the double quotation. Readers familiar with Roman Imperial propaganda would hardly miss the parallels to the Priene Inscription. More eagle-eyed readers may have noticed the similarities to the opening of the Pauline epistles. Mark's text both incorporates and transforms older texts while challenging the present order of things. Along with this is the subtle recognition of Christianity's first literary heavyweight. Rather than merely stitching texts together, Mark subtly weaves them in order to create a rich and layered text.

REVELATION (1 COR 1:4–9 AND MARK 1:9–11)

This section of 1 Corinthians fulfils the standard Hellenistic letter function of a thanksgiving. However, Paul goes far beyond this basic function. He discusses the grace of God which he sees as given to the Corinthians in the form of Jesus. Paul also mentions spiritual gifts which will become a major theme later in the letter as well as the calling of the Corinthians which will be met again at the end of chapter 1.

---

21. Nelis, *Vergil's Aeneid*, 5.
22. Thomas, *Reading Virgil*, 253.

Comparison and Analysis of 1 Corinthians 1–2 and Mark 1:1–28

In Mark 1:9–11 Jesus appears and is baptized by John in the Jordan. During the baptism the sky is ripped open and the spirit descends into Jesus and a voice from the sky speaks and calls Jesus 'my beloved son.' The voice is pleased with Jesus and this is his first appearance in the narrative.

Initial General Comparison

When comparing these two texts, the following general observations can be made. Both texts build up to a revelation. In 1 Cor 1:4–9 Paul gives thanks for the Corinthians and the grace that has been given to them by God. The purpose of this, Paul reveals, is that when Jesus is 'revealed' they will not be lacking in spiritual gifts. In Mark there is also a revelation which is the culmination of the baptism episode. During the baptism, the skies rip apart and a voice reveals that Jesus is the son of God. It is also learned that the Corinthians will become blameless while Jesus is announced as the beloved.

However, there are also many differences that cannot be ignored. Both texts have different functions on a superficial level. First Corinthians 1:4–9 looks like a simple thanksgiving before Paul begins the main arguments of his letter. Mark 1:9–11 is introducing Jesus to the reader/hearers of the gospel in person. It is part of a narrative flow with certain characters, location and a timeframe. First Corinthians 1:4–9 is certainly not a scene like Mark 1:9–11.

Literary Aspects of Mark 1:9–11

Parallels with Other Texts

OLD TESTAMENT

According to Collins, the Markan baptism may incorporate Isa 61:1–2, which describes the Spirit as bring given, as a possible source. The fact that Mark mentions and quotes Isaiah at the beginning of the gospel makes literary dependence here more likely. The quote (Mark 1:2–3) also suggests that Jesus and John have been prefigured and, if this baptism text (Mark 1:10) is indeed modelled on Isa 61:1–2, it suggests that the baptism is also prefigured by Isaiah.[23]

23. Collins, *Mark,* 149.

The Quest for Mark's Sources

The Markan baptism may also have used Ps 2:7 and Gen 1:2.²⁴ Psalm 2:7 contains the phrase με Υἱός μου εἶ σύ, ἐγὼ σήμερον γεγέννηκά σε·, which is very similar to the voice from heaven in Mark 1:11. In Gen 1:2 the spirit of God is said to hover, or be over the waters, and this brings images of birds to mind. Mark has an affinity with all three texts (Isa 61:1–2; Ps 2:7; and Gen 1:2) and continues the level of intertextuality that was observed in Mark 1:1–3.²⁵ The reader can be left with no doubt that this text will overtly and subtly interweave texts.

Apocrypha

The apocryphal *Joseph and Aseneth*²⁶ may provide a background to the unusual phrase σχιζομένους τοὺς οὐρανοὺς in Mark 1:10. There is no precedence for this phrase in the LXX where ἀνοιγω is the more commonly used verb to describe the opening of the heavens.²⁷ The *Joseph and Aseneth* text contains a similar phrase to Mark 1:10 and uses the same verb. The text reads ἐσχίσθη ὁ οὐρανος and this appears to be the only similar phrase that possibly predates Mark. In *Joseph and Aseneth* the heavens are split near the morning star, a great light appears and an angel descends from heaven.²⁸ In Mark, a voice, as opposed to light, is heard and the Spirit descends, rather than an angel. Nevertheless, the parallels are striking.

Classical Texts

The possible influence of classical literature here must also be recognized, particularly in the descent of the spirit. The descent of a god to earth to deliver a message is a common motif in epic literature. In the *Iliad*, many gods descend from Olympus to Troy with the purpose of aiding, hindering and delivering messages to heroes. This motif appears, to a lesser degree, in

---

24. Ibid. See also, Marcus, *Mark*, 1:159.

25. Ibid.

26. This apocryphal text is usually dated to the first century B.C.E. although dates into the second century C.E. have been suggested, making Markan dependence on this text impossible. The idea that Mark may be using this text is pure speculation. See Collins, *Mark*, 148.

27. See Isa 63:19 and Ezek 1:1. For more detailed discussion see, Collins, *Mark*, 148.

28. Ibid.

Comparison and Analysis of 1 Corinthians 1–2 and Mark 1:1–28

the *Odyssey* and is imitated by both Virgil and Ovid.[29] Homer often uses the image of a bird to describe this descent.[30] E. P. Dixon has argued that Homeric literature undoubtedly has influenced the Markan baptism and argues that Mark's audience, whether Jewish, Greek, Roman, or a mixture could not have failed to spot the Homeric images.[31]

The combination of Homeric and Old Testament material is not problematic. There is no reason why both could not have been used as ". . .the identity of Jesus was communicated by and to individuals from diverse backgrounds."[32] Dixon goes on to say

> The Spirit's "descent as a dove" suggests the presence of a Homeric literary motif in Mark's baptism account. Such an interpretation by no means intends to suppress the Jewish characteristics of the Markan baptism. The report certainly draws images from the OT as well.[33]

Detailed Comparison

Context

The context of 1 Cor 1:4–9 is Paul's progressing argument. He has now finished with the formal introductions and begins to prepare for his main theological arguments in the first two chapters. Following this section Paul will then begin to discuss the divisions amongst the Corinthian church. This section, therefore, serves as a transition between the letter opening and the main arguments of the letter. In Mark 1:9–11 Jesus is being baptized. This is the first appearance of Jesus in the gospel. Following this Jesus will be cast out into the wilderness to be tempted by Satan. Like 1 Cor 1:4–9 this passage serves as a transition. The transition here is between the activity of John the Baptist and the beginning of the ministry of Jesus of Nazareth. This section serves to figuratively pass the torch from one to the other. Both texts, therefore, have an introductory role.

---

29. Thomas M. Greene has carried out a full study of the motive of the divine descent in epic poetry from Homer to Milton. See, Greene, *Descent From Heaven*.

30. For example, see *Il.* 13:62–65; 15:237–38; 18:616–17; 19:349–350. *Od.* 1:320; 3:371–72. Virgil also imitates this image at *Aen.* 4:238–61 and 9:18–22.

31. Dixon, "Descending Spirit," 75–80.

32. Ibid., 770.

33. Ibid., 779.

Theme

This section of 1 Corinthians serves to bring Paul's focus on the Corinthians, just as Mark draws attention to Jesus. The mention of revelation in 1 Cor 1:7 (ἀποκάλυψιν) may be significant. There is also a revelation in Mark during the baptism of Jesus who is proclaimed the son of God by a voice coming out of the sky. It is unclear whether this is a revelation to Jesus alone, John the Baptist, or all of the people present at this scene but for whoever the revelation is intended, it is a revelation nonetheless. Just as the mention of revelation in 1 Cor 1:7 signifies that revelation will be an important part of Paul's letter, so too in Mark this is the first part of a cycle of revelations that will culminate in the revelation of the centurion at the crucifixion.[34] Paul writes of the Corinthians waiting for the revealing of Jesus Christ while in Mark it is Jesus who is revealed to be the Son of God.

Both texts identify Jesus as the Son of God (1 Cor 1:9; Mark 1:11; and earlier in Mark 1:1). However, this is universal to all New Testament texts. Also, the voice from the heavens speaks of being pleased with Jesus and Paul is pleased with the Corinthians. He expresses this by giving thanks to God for them (Εὐχαριστῶ—I give thanks). This mirrors the pleasure of the voice with Jesus during the baptism (εὐδόκησα—I am well pleased).

Another small connection comes in the form of a spiritual call. Jesus' baptism is a scene in the vein of Old Testament commissioning scenes.[35] This call is carried out through anointing or baptism. In 1 Cor 1:9 Paul reminds the Corinthians that they were called to fellowship in Jesus Christ (this call will become important again later in 1 Cor 1–2). Baptism, as will become apparent, is key in this calling and fellowship. In Mark, Jesus is called and in 1 Corinthians people are called to him.

A final theme that emerges is the theme of giving gifts. In 1 Cor 1:7 Paul speaks of the many spiritual gifts the Corinthians have received. Spiritual gifts and divine sonship is a motif that is found many times in the letters of Paul. It is found in Gal 4:6; 5:22; Rom 8:14–22; and again in 1 Cor 12:7–11. In Mark 1:10–11 the spirit descends into Jesus who is then called Son. It is significant that the references to spiritual gifts and divine sonship are found together in close proximity in these two sections of 1 Corinthians and Mark. The abundance of gifts in 1 Cor 1:4–7 is associated with the Spirit and God's son and is matched in Mark 1:9–11 by the descent of the

---

34. Ibid.
35. Dowd, *Reading Mark*, 11. Isa 61:1 is such a scene.

Comparison and Analysis of 1 Corinthians 1–2 and Mark 1:1–28

Spirit into Jesus and the declaration of his divine sonship. In both texts this is accompanied by an expression of approval; thanks in 1 Corinthians and being well pleased in Mark.

Action/Plot and Order

In terms of action/plot the differing genres make connections unlikely. Narratives and letters progress in different fashions and little is found. However, certain similarities are present. Revelation is present in both and in 1 Corinthians it is a future revelation of the blameless while in Mark it is a past revelation of the beloved. Paul looks ahead while Mark looks back. The action is reversed in Mark when compared to 1 Corinthians in terms of time, and there is a variation from a group to a person.

Vocabulary

The vocabulary similarities between these two sections are small but worth noting. Both sections use the word ἡμέρα. Paul uses the phrase ἐν τῇ ἡμέρᾳ. Mark uses a similar phrase ἐν ἐκείναις ταῖς ἡμέραις (v9), variations of which can be found throughout the LXX.[36] Both use the similar phrase in terms of Jesus. Paul is looking forward while Mark is looking back. The use of υἱός is also similar in both. In 1 Cor 1:8 Paul describes Jesus as υἱοῦ αὐτοῦ (his son) while in Mark, Jesus is described as υἱός μου (my son).

While not exact there is a certain affinity between the use of εὐχαπιστέω in 1 Cor 1:4 and εὐδοκέω in Mark 1:11. Both convey a sense of pleasure. Paul is giving thanks to God, while in Mark it is God who is pleased with Jesus. Also the words ἀνέγκλητος (1 Cor 1:8) and ἀγαπητός (Mark 1:14) have an overlap of meaning. Someone who is blameless could be said to be beloved.

Assessment and Conclusion

When all of the data collected is put together a picture of Mark as a complex gospel with many sources carefully woven together begins to emerge. Mark has consistently woven Old Testament texts together in the composition of the gospel, while possibly making use of classical texts. In addition there

---

36. For example, see Exod 2:11; Judg 18:31; and 1 Sam 28:1 (all LXX).

are some affinities with 1 Cor 1:4–9. The similarities between these two sections can be summarized as follows:

- Both come near the beginning of their respective documents and both set out the key players of the texts—the Corinthians and Jesus.
- Both focus on a distant time. Paul looks to the future revelation of the blameless (ἀνέγκλητος) while Mark looks back to the revelation of the beloved (ἀγαπητός).
- Both show expressions of being pleased, expressed to/by God. In 1 Cor 1:4–9 this occurs at the very beginning of the section while in Mark 1:9–11 this occurs at the very end of the section (1 Cor 1:4; Mark 1:11).
- Gifts are bestowed in each. Paul speaks of the gifts associated with the Spirit while the Spirit descends into Jesus in Mark.
- Revelation is the climactic core of both sections.
- In both texts revelation involves Jesus' role as God's son.

How then is this to be interpreted? In terms of trying to explain these similarities two possible explanations present themselves. The first is that these parallels are mere coincidence. Could the affinities noted be there by pure chance with no literary connection whatsoever? If there was only one similarity then this argument could be made. However, there are multiple similarities in a small body of text. Coincidence, therefore, becomes much more unlikely, particularly when it is considered that these similarities are part of a larger chain. The other possibility is that 1 Cor 1:4–9 has been woven into the fabric of Mark 1:9–11 in a fashion that is significantly similar to the way poets of the ancient world interwove texts. It is in this latter explanation that these similarities can be understood. First Corinthians, therefore, can be understood as one component of Mark which is also informed by many other texts.

FOURFOLD DIVISION/UNITY (1 COR 1:10–13 AND MARK 1:16–20)

These sections both deal with division and unity. First Corinthians 1:10–13 deals with the divisions that have emerged in Corinth. Four factions have emerged, all aligned with a different person. Paul raises the issue of baptism which will also become a major theme.

In Mark 1:16–20 Jesus begins to call disciples to him. Firstly he calls Simon and Andrew who are fishing. Jesus calls them and they immediately follow. Next he calls James and John who are with their father mending nets. Again, Jesus calls and they follow.

Initial General Comparison

When comparing these two texts one obvious similarity that presents itself is the motif of brothers. Paul speaks to the brothers of the Corinthian church while in Mark Jesus encounters two sets of brothers. Another theme that appears is unity. Unity is an issue in Corinth as the community has divided itself into factions, while in Mark the brothers are united in following Jesus.

A key issue in both texts is the way in which adherence to the word of Jesus brings unity. Paul calls for unity based on Jesus' name and the crucifixion. He highlights that not focusing on Jesus has led to divisions amongst the Corinthian community. Mark, on the other hand, shows a variation of this. He shows the harmony and unity that follows when Jesus is listened to.

Literary Aspects of Mark 1:16–20

Parallels with Other Texts

OLD TESTAMENT

An influence from 1 Kings can be seen here as the call of Elisha is generally regarded as providing a literary model, or at least a partial model, for this section of Mark.[37] The two texts of 1 Kgs 19:19–21 and Mark 1:16–18 share little in vocabulary but do share many elements of plot. First Kings 19:19–21 has three basic plot points which are then incorporated into Mark.[38] These are:

- Elijah passes by Elisha.
- Elijah casts his cloak over Elisha which signifies that Elisha should follow Elijah and then become his successor.
- Elisha follows Elijah after kissing his parents, presumably goodbye.

---

37. Marcus, *Mark*, 1:183.
38. Ibid.

The Quest for Mark's Sources

When looking at Mark 1:16–20 all of these plot points have been incorporated into the call of the disciples and repeated, thus amplifying the source text.

- Jesus passes along the Sea of Galilee and sees Simon and Andrew.
- Jesus instructs them to follow.
- They follow.

  Repeated cycle of plot points:
- Jesus moves along further.
- He calls to James and John.
- They follow.

Mark intensifies the action of 1 Kings by repeating it. Jesus is presented as being more powerful than Elijah. Jesus does not need to cast a cloak and the disciples just drop what they are doing and follow him. None of the disciples ask permission from their relatives to leave. In the case of James and John their father is present and is merely left in the boat. The call of Elisha provided Mark with a ready-made model for the call of these first disciples and it provides much of the plot.[39]

Detailed Comparison

Context

In terms of the context of each section within their respective texts there is little to be said in terms of similarities.

Theme

In this section Paul moves on first to emphasize unity and then to discuss factionalism within the Corinthian church. He mentions four factions that have emerged.[40] These are the factions belonging to Paul, Apollos, Peter,

---

39. For an in-depth and recent discussion of the relationship between Mark 1:1–20 and the Elijah-Elisha narrative see, Winn, *Elijah-Elisha*, 69–76. Winn proposes that the author of Mark systematically used the Elijah-Elisha narrative as a literary source using Greco-Roman literary techniques.

40. Both Fitzmyer and Conzelmann have noted that Paul may only be speaking of three factions here as opposed to four, which is what most commentators assume. Fitzmyer argues that there may be three factions and that the people who find such factions trivial are only loyal to Christ. Conzelmann, on the other hand, has argued that Ἐγὼ

Comparison and Analysis of 1 Corinthians 1–2 and Mark 1:1–28

and Christ. Mark, on the other hand, mentions four disciples that join Jesus, namely the brothers Simon and Andrew and the brothers James and John. When looking closely at these texts the scene in Mark is the opposite of the situation in 1 Corinthians. Paul speaks of a four-fold division. The Corinthian church is in a state of utter turmoil as the people are quarrelling over who they "belong to" which led to growing factionalism among the early Christians in Corinth. Mark, on the other hand, presents a four-fold unity. Jesus calls four disciples who calmly leave what they are doing and follow him. There is no mention of any conflict, nor is there mention of any divisions or factionalism amongst the four. Thus, instead of having divisions (σχίσματα—1 Cor 1:10), they are united in following Jesus (ἠκολούθησαν αὐτῷ—Mark 1:18). The scene is one of calm and unity—a sharp contrast to the picture painted by Paul.

Action/Plot and Order

The differing genres of 1 Corinthians and Mark make similarities of action/plot unlikely. The two genres function in different ways. Mark is a story while 1 Corinthians does not follow a narrative structure. Yet, there is a central point of similarity. This is to do with the disunity/unity theme in both sections. In 1 Cor 1:10–13 four factions are in a state of disunity and Paul asks them to mend themselves (κατηρτισμένοι) while in Mark the polar opposite is found. Four brothers (two sets—a pattern different from 1 Corinthians) are found in a state of unity, and two of them are mending nets (καταρτίζοντας) and they follow Jesus in the correct manner.[41] This may not appear to be a similarity at all as the situation of unity in Mark is the opposite of the disunity in Corinth. However, the contrast is so precise that it constitutes a significant connection and it is understandable as deliberate on Mark's part—as a way of presenting an opposing or ideal situation to that in Corinth. The reason for this could be pedagogical in that Mark is demonstrating the correct way to respond to Jesus' call. This process of reversal was a common literary technique in both Jewish and Greco-Roman

---

δὲ Χριστοῦ (v. 12) may be a statement by Paul on his own beliefs and that he is merely stating that he, himself, belongs to Christ. Whatever the amount of groups there were in Corinth, what is important for the present purpose is that four names are mentioned in 1 Corinthians and in Mark both, and this is how the writer of Mark may have interpreted the text. See Fitzmyer, *First Corinthians,* 137, and Conzelmann, *1 Corinthians,* 33.

41. It has already been noted that the number of factions in 1 Corinthians is disputed. For the sake of argument, four factions will be assumed in the present case.

literature. In this instance the use of the rare verb καταρτίζω along with the four factions/brothers makes a dramatic reversal more likely.

In terms of order there is little beyond the continuing similarities found between 1 Cor 1–2 and Mark 1:1–28.

Vocabulary

The vocabulary links here are small but two words, in particular, deserve note. The shared use of the verb καταρτίζω is significant because of its sparse use in the New Testament. It essentially means to mend but has connotations of putting things in order, restoring and making things complete. The verb appears in 1 Cor 1:10 and Mark 1:19. In the LXX the verb only appears in Ezra[42] and various Psalms[43] while in the New Testament it is essentially a Pauline verb. The verb appears thirteen times in the New Testament and eight of these occurrences are in Paul's letters. It appears twice in Matthew, with one being sourced from Mark, and appears once in Mark and Luke and once in 1 Peter. This is, therefore, a rare word and it occurs in close proximity to two instances of the noun ἀδελφός. It also occurs in 1 Corinthians and Mark in the context of unity—ἦτε δὲ κατηρτισμένοι ἐν τῷ αὐτῷ νοΐ (1 Cor 1:10) and, καὶ αὐτοὺς ἐν τῷ πλοίῳ καταρτίζοντας τὰ δίκτυα (Mark 1:19). In 2 Cor 13:11 ἀδελφός is also found near καταρτίζω as it does in this section of 1 Corinthians. This passage is quite similar to 1 Cor 1:10. In both, Paul is appealing to the Corinthian church to agree with one another.

Completeness

In these sections it can be seen that many of the major elements of 1 Cor 1:10–13 are found in Mark 1:16–20 including the use of ἀδελφός and καταρτίζω as well as the theme of unity and the appearance of four factions/brothers. This continues the chain of similarities noted from the start of 1 Corinthians. The elements of Mark that do not match with 1 Corinthians can be accounted for, largely, by appealing to 1 Kings.

---

42. Ezra 4:12, 13, 16; 5:3, 9, 11; 6:14.
43. Pss 8:3; 10:3; 16:5; 17:34; 28:9; 39:7; 67:10; 73:16; 79:16; 88:38.

Comparison and Analysis of 1 Corinthians 1–2 and Mark 1:1–28

Assessment and Conclusion

In conclusion, many connections can be found between these two sections and these can be summarized as follows:

- Paul appeals for unity and describes factionalism and disunity in Corinth while Mark creates a scene of unity amongst the first followers of Jesus in a case of dramatic reversal.
- Both use ἀδελφός twice. While this is not significant as it is a very common noun, it highlights a central aspect of both texts.
- Both portray disunity/unity with four distinct names—a relatively unusual feature.
- Both texts use the verb καταρτίζω which is an uncommon verb.

Also, as has been seen, Mark looks like a reversal. Mark is presenting an ideal; an example of how to correctly respond to Jesus' call, something to which the Corinthians do not. The texts are complementary in that Paul presents a problem while Mark shows the solutions.

In Mark, 1 Kgs 1:19–21 forms the core source of the narrative. It also determines the structure of the narrative. But Mark also has similarities with 1 Cor 1:10–13. If just one of these similarities were present then it could be ascribed to coincidence. However, there are many similarities which form a chain that extends from the start of each text. Distillation and *contaminatio* are the best ways to explain this. The story of Jesus' earthly ministry has been pinned onto the underlying framework of 1 Kgs 1:19–21 and enriched with strands of 1 Cor 1:10–13. Mark can be seen as a much layered text pulling strands from multiple sources. Within this process 1 Cor 1:10–13 appears, in this instance, to be one component of Mark's narrative.

BAPTISM (1 COR 1:14–17 AND MARK 1:4–8)

In 1 Cor 1:14–17 Paul discusses his baptizing activity from when he was in Corinth. He refutes the notion that he was baptizing people in his own name. He states that he was not sent by Christ to baptize but rather to preach the good news. The power of the cross is also mentioned here, which is a continuing and important theme.

In Mark 1:4–8 John the Baptist appears in the wilderness and begins to baptize people in the Jordan. John is described and he says that one is coming who will baptize the people in the Holy Spirit.

Initial General Comparison

When looking at the two texts, the shared theme of baptism is immediately obvious and, as would be expected, many uses of the verb βαπτίζω are found clustered together. Paul wants to go beyond baptizing and to a different level. He wants to preach the message of the cross of Christ. Similarly, in Mark, John too goes beyond baptizing and to another level. His focus is also on preaching as he speaks of the more powerful one to come who will not baptize with water but with the Holy Spirit. While baptism is the starting point for both, they go beyond this and move to a deeper message about Christ in Paul, and someone more powerful in Mark.

Literary Aspects of Mark 1:4–8

Parallels with Other Texts.

Old Testament

As with the previous sections there is also a strong connection to the Elijah-Elisha narrative in 1 and 2 Kings. John the Baptist is presented as the second Elijah who is described in very similar terms. In 2 Kgs 1:8 Elijah is described as being a hairy man with a leather belt. John the Baptist is described as wearing camel hair with a leather belt. Marcus sees a possible influence from Zechariah here where prophets are described as wearing hairy mantles.[44] John the Baptist is clearly cast in the role of the Old Testament prophet and Elijah appears to be at the core of this. There is also a connection to Elisha here. Both Elisha and John are connected with the river Jordan. This is where John baptizes and it is where Elisha sends Naaman to be restored in 2 Kgs 5:10 by being immersed (βαπτίζω—2 Kgs 5:14). This is one of only four uses of βαπτίζω in the LXX. It also features prominently in the story of Elijah's ascension and the passing on of the prophetic gift to Elisha in 2 Kings 2. Given that Elijah was expected to return before the

---

44. Marcus, *Mark*, 1:156. Zech 13:4 (LXX).

messiah, the connection to John the Baptist makes perfect sense.[45] First and Second Kings presents itself as a major component of Mark early on in the gospel.

Detailed Comparison

Context

In 1 Corinthians the description of Paul's baptizing activity comes straight after his opening discussion about the factionalism within the Corinthian church. Baptism is introduced much later in the text than it is in Mark where the first mention of baptism comes straight after the conflated Old Testament quote in Mark 1:2–3. They both, however, form a prelude to a major statement about Jesus (about crucifixion and about his identity as God's son). However, context offers little for discussion at this point.

Theme

Baptism is the initial theme of both sections. Paul mentions that he only baptized a few people in Corinth and is glad that he did not baptize others as he does not want people saying they were baptized in his own name. The baptizing is kept to a minimum. He also wants to move away from this and onto other things. In Mark, however, "people from the whole Judean countryside and all the people of Jerusalem" are being baptized by John the Baptist. John is defined by his baptism to such an extent that he is introduced with the epithet ὁ βαπτίζων in v4. However, like Paul, John also moves onto other things. Both texts involve preaching that is centered on Christ, on the cross in 1 Cor 1:17 and on his baptizing with the Holy Spirit in Mark 1:8.

Action/Plot and Order

The basic action/plot in these two sections is similar. At the center of both is the image of someone baptizing others. Both baptize followers and both have a preaching aspect connected to this which puts the emphasis on Jesus. There is, however, a reversal as the actions moves from the few, in Paul, to the many, in Mark, and again from chaos to peace between the two texts.

---

45. For example, see Mal 3:22 (LXX).

Vocabulary

The sections share a repeated use of the verb βαπτίζω which holds the discussion about baptism together in both texts. The use of βαπτίζω occurs many times throughout 1 Cor 1–2 and Mark1:1–28 and is found clustered in the two sections being analyzed here.

This is the only such cluster in Paul although another cluster is found in Mark 10:38–39. Other such clusters can be found throughout the New Testament.[46] While these clusters are fairly common to the New Testament (especially in the gospels and Acts) they are not to the LXX where the verb only occurs four times.[47] The clusters found in the relevant sections of 1 Corinthians and Mark need to be viewed as part of the growing chain of similarities that is emerging.

Completeness

In terms of completeness, most of the elements of this small section of 1 Corinthians find a parallel in Mark 1:4–8. It is, however, spread out over a much larger section in Mark. Baptism is the core theme of both texts and there are certain plot points that connect them also. However, this needs to be taken along with the previous sections which also showed that most of the elements of 1 Cor 1–2 have parallels in Mark 1:1–28.

Assessment and Conclusion

The similarities between these two sections are clear and can be summarized as follows:

- Baptism permeates and dominates these texts as shown by the repeated use in both of βαπτίζω.
- Paul and John not only baptize but they also preach.
- The preaching is focused towards Jesus on a level well beyond baptizing. Paul introduces the power of the cross while John says that the one who is stronger will baptize with the Holy Spirit.

---

46. Matt 3 has six usages. Luke 3 also uses the verb six times. John 1 and 3 contain clusters of βαπτίζω as does Acts 8, 16 and 19. By "cluster" more than two usages of a verb in close proximity is meant.

47. 2 Kgs 5:14; Judg 12:7; Sir 34:25; and Isa 21:4.

Comparison and Analysis of 1 Corinthians 1–2 and Mark 1:1–28

Mark has a strong dependence on 1 and 2 Kings in this section and while they are not Mark's only Old Testament sources, it is a major one and appears to be, in certain sections, a key element of the framework around which Mark composed his narrative. It is within the framework of Mark's reliance on Old Testament texts that these similarities with 1 Corinthians need to be understood. Also, at the base of Mark's text is a narrative about the life and ministry of Jesus of Nazareth and this is something which is not underlying 1 Corinthians. The similarities noted between 1 Cor 1:14–17 and Mark 1:4–8 do not account for all the data in Mark. However, they do match some significant components of this section of Mark.

PROCLAIMING AND POWER (1 COR 1:18–25 AND MARK 1:14–15)

In this section Paul discusses the power and wisdom of God which he views as being the cross. To the Greeks this is folly and to the Jews, a stumbling block, according to Paul. He concludes this section by saying that God's foolishness and weakness is above man's wisdom and strength. In Mark 1:14–15 Jesus begins his ministry by going to Galilee to preach the gospel. He asks people to repent and hear the good news.

Initial General Comparison

At first these texts look very different. First Corinthians 1:18–25 is a much longer theological argument while Mark 1:14–15 is two verses of a progressing narrative. Paul goes into a detailed theological argument about the power and wisdom of the cross while Mark describes, briefly, Jesus' emergence from the wilderness and the beginning of his ministry.

The general theme that presents itself when comparing these two sections is one of preaching, in particular a new form of preaching that challenges the prevailing mindset. Paul is preaching about the power of the cross which began in 1 Cor 1:17, while in Mark, Jesus is conducting the first preaching of his ministry. Both proclamations emphasize the need for a change of mind. For Paul, the cross is at the center of this change. Through the cross, in Paul's view, God has made foolish the wisdom of "this age." Similarly in Mark, Jesus also challenges the present age by asking people to repent and by proclaiming the kingdom of God.

The Quest for Mark's Sources
Literary Aspects of Mark 1:14–15

Parallels with Other Texts

OLD TESTAMENT

Unusually, little Old Testament connections can be found here. The passage does evoke images of Old Testament prophets, particularly Elijah who was connected with the wilderness. The idea of fulfilling time is a theme very much present in the Old Testament and is something which New Testament texts regularly appeal to in their characterization of Jesus and Mark often presents Jesus as the fulfilment of the Old Testament.

One text, again from the Elijah-Elisha narrative, may provide a background to this portion of Mark and that is 1 Kgs 19:15–18. In this text Jehu is designated as the king of Israel by God and Elisha is named as Elijah's successor. Jehu is seen as the one who will restore God's kingdom. Winn sees Mark 1:14–15 as an imitation of 1 Kgs 19:15–18.[48] Although he recognizes the similarities are less specific than in other cases, Winn argues that the case for literary dependence is still plausible because of stronger similarities in other areas.[49] This is a significant claim as it does not rely on common vocabulary. It relies on strong thematic similarities, as does the proposed reliance on 1 Corinthians presented here. Also, Winn's example shows that when a similarity is not specific in nature it can still contribute to a case for literary dependence if it is part of a string of similarities.

NEW TESTAMENT

Marcus has identified Mark 1:14–15 as being a possible baptism formula and has compared it to other New Testament baptism formulae in the Pauline corpus, namely Rom 13:12; 1 Thess 5:5–6; and Col 1:13.[50] In the case of Mark 1:14–15 and Rom 13:12 these similarities follow the same order namely: ". . . (1) announcement of the termination of the old age, (2) announcement of the beginning of the new age, (3) call to turn away from the old age, and (4) call to turn toward the new age."[51] Marcus provides a table in which he compares all these similar texts line by line and they are

---

48. Winn, *Elijah-Elisha*, 73.
49. Ibid., 1:174.
50. Marcus, *Mark*, 1:174.
51. Ibid.

all indeed similar. Therefore, as with Mark 1:1–3 there is another instance of there being a possible connection to other letters as opposed to just 1 Corinthians.

Detailed Comparison

Context

First Corinthians 1:18–25 follows on from Paul's discussion of his baptizing activity. He initially started by talking about baptism in v14 but then shifts focus to the power of the cross in v18. Mark, too, shifts focus from Jesus' baptism and temptation and turns to the start of Jesus' ministry when he emerges from the wilderness. The baptism and temptation are somewhat preamble to the start of Jesus' ministry, just as baptism was a way for Paul to introduce his discussion of the power of the cross. Following this in 1 Cor 1:26–31, Paul will ask the Corinthians to consider their own call while in Mark, Jesus will go on to call his first followers. This, then, is the context of these two sections within their own texts and again it offers little for the discussion of literary dependence.

Theme

This section of 1 Corinthians shares some similarities with the corresponding section in Mark and these are the themes of preaching and believing in the context of a challenge to the prevailing mindset. Paul sees the cross as a challenge to the present order and mindset. The way to respond to the cross is with a change of mind. Likewise in Mark, Jesus calls for a change of heart/mind and proclaims the kingdom of God (ἡ βασιλεία τοῦ θεοῦ).

Another very small connection may be found in 1 Cor 1:20 and Mark 1:15. Paul asks ποῦ συζητητὴς τοῦ αἰῶνος τούτου; (1 Cor 1:20) whereas Mark has Jesus say: Πεπλήρωται ὁ καιρὸς (Mark 1:15). Both are concerned with time although in different ways. Paul is concerned with the present while Mark is focused on the ending of the present time and the establishment of the ἡ βασιλεία τοῦ θεοῦ.

Action/Plot and Order

In spite of the large size difference between these two sections some elements of action/plot from 1 Cor 1:18–25 can be found in Mark 1:14–15. Firstly, both Paul and Jesus are proclaiming and evangelizing. Paul proclaims Christ crucified while in Mark, Jesus is proclaiming the good news. Both have a focus on time as well. Paul is concerned with "this age" while in Mark, Jesus speaks of time being fulfilled.

However, Paul's main focus here is on the cross and the word "cross" is absent in Mark 1:14–15. This is not surprising. Mark is presenting a narrative of the life of Jesus and, therefore, presents this in a chronological fashion meaning that the cross is not introduced until much later in the gospel. However, Paul defined the cross as the power of God and Mark matches this emphasis on the power of God with the central phrase, the kingdom of God (Mark 1:15). The cross and the arrival of a new age in 1 Cor 1:18–25 is matched in Mark by the message about the coming kingdom of God, which will also be a new age. The word/message of the cross is the power of God for Paul and later in Mark the cross is the beginning of the establishment of the kingdom of God. In terms of order, these sections offer little.

Vocabulary

Only two words are shared in these two sections, namely πιστεύω and κηρύσσω. While these two words are common verbs, they do reveal some of the themes noted in these sections.

Completeness

In terms of completeness essentially all of the elements of 1 Cor 1:18–25 find a parallel in Mark 1:14–15. The word "cross" is absent in this section of Mark, but the cross is described as the power of God and its equivalent is found in Mark in the form of the kingdom of God. Faith, preaching, change of mindset and fulfilment of time are all found in Mark in a distilled form.

Comparison and Analysis of 1 Corinthians 1–2 and Mark 1:1–28

Assessment and Conclusion

There is a certain difficulty in assessing the evidence collected for these two sections. The difference in size makes it hard to assess what is going on, yet the links are as follows:

- Both have explicit emphasis on preaching.
- Both emphasize something powerful, challenging the present age. For Paul this is the cross, the power of God, and for Mark it is the kingdom of God.
- Both emphasize faith.
- Both focus on aspects of time.
- Both call for a change of mind.

Is this coincidence? Or are these elements being distilled in Mark into two short verses? This technique of distillation was a common one in the ancient world and allowed a writer to present parts of a larger text in a much smaller space.

Only one other possible source was found for this section of Mark, namely 1 Kgs 19:15–18, where God effectively announces to Elisha that a new order is coming with two new kings, and it appears as if this was used in much the same way as 1 Cor 1:18–25. This is significant as it provides precedence within Mark of this type of usage. This style of textual weaving and absorption was common in the ancient world, especially amongst Greek and Latin poets. It is within this framework that these parallels need to be understood.

TAKING A CRITICAL LOOK AT THE CALL (1 COR 1:26–31 AND MARK 1:12–13)

Paul asks the Corinthians in 1 Cor 1:26–31, to consider their own call and points out that not many of them were wise or of noble birth. Paul uses this to prove the point that he made in the previous section about God choosing what appears to be weak and foolish in order to show wisdom and power. In Mark 1:12–13, immediately following the baptism, Jesus is cast out into the wilderness by the Spirit and is tempted by Satan for forty days.

The Quest for Mark's Sources

Initial General Comparison

Unlike the sections already analyzed these two texts present no obvious similarities. One thematic affinity that does present itself is the religious call. As in the previous section there is a large difference in size between the two texts.

Literary Aspects of Mark 1:12–13

Parallels with other texts.

OLD TESTAMENT

Again multiple connections to the Elijah-Elisha narrative are found. The verb, ἐκβάλλω, meaning to cast out, evokes images of Elijah being transported by the spirit of the Lord in 1 Kgs 18:12 and 2 Kgs 2:16, although different verbs are used.[52] The forty days that Jesus spends in the wilderness may be influenced by 1 Kgs 19:5–8 where Elijah spends the same amount of time there and is also aided by an angel.[53] Moses, too, spends forty days on Sinai in Exod 24:18. Both of these texts are likely to have influenced Mark.

Detailed Comparison

Context

This section of 1 Cor 1–2 follows on from Paul's discussion of the wisdom and power of God and comes before the largest of the sub-units, 1 Cor 2. This section sees a shift from the general discussion of the situation in Corinth and turns the focus onto the Corinthians themselves. Here, all introduction is left behind. Similarly, in Mark, the focus has changed. The preceding unit sees the narrative shift from John to Jesus and this is continued in Jesus' Temptation. Following this Jesus will go on to begin his ministry. Both units sit at pivotal points early within their respective documents.

---

52. Marcus, *Mark*, 1:167.
53. Winn, *Elijah-Elisha*, 71–73.

Comparison and Analysis of 1 Corinthians 1–2 and Mark 1:1–28

Theme

In 1 Cor 1:26–31 Paul is asking the Corinthians to look at their call and to face the full reality of it. In the corresponding section of Mark, Jesus is in the wilderness after his dramatic baptism. In essence, after a spectacular baptism where God speaks directly to him from the sky, Jesus is cast into the wilderness being brought back down to earth and reminded of his humanity. He is being tempted by Satan, showing that he is prone to the same frailties and temptations as everybody else. Paul is reminding the Corinthians that they are ordinary people and, like Jesus during the temptation, they need to look at and test their call.

Action/Plot and Order

In terms of action/plot both texts share an elevated call followed by an immediate testing and examination. In terms of order, there is little to discuss.

Vocabulary

These two sections share no significant vocabulary. However, there is an interesting parallel in terms of vocabulary with another part of 1 Corinthians. In 1 Cor 7:5 there is a phrase very similar to πειραζόμενος ὑπὸ τοῦ Σατανᾶ (tempted by Satan—Mark 1:13). While discussing marriage and conjugal rights, Paul emphasizes self control so that Satan will not tempt them (ἵνα μὴ πειράζῃ ὑμᾶς ὁ Σατανᾶς—1 Cor 7:5). This is very similar to the passage found in Mark and is the only time that the verb πειράζω is used along with σατάν in the New Testament or LXX.

Assessment and Conclusion

When it comes to putting the collected data together, this section is puzzling. No vocabulary is shared and only thematic links can be found based around people being brought low and humbled. It is also possible to view both as being a spiritual call. Mark's clearest dependence here is on part of 1 and 2 Kings. Underneath this is Mark's basic narrative about the ministry of Jesus. With no verbal agreement between these two sections a direct link cannot be made. Nevertheless, there is a certain thematic affinity—the down to earth examining or testing of a high call, a testing in which those who are called are reminded that they are weak and vulnerable. There is no place for boasting in Corinth and none in the desert. Both share affinities in this regard.

On the verbal level, the presence of the reference in 1 Cor 7 to being tempted by Satan is significant. Apart from the Markan Temptation it is the only time in the LXX or New Testament that the word πειράζω is used along with σατάν. Mark's account of the temptation shares a unique connection with the larger text of 1 Corinthians. In other words, in the Markan text which at first sight has no verbal link with 1 Corinthians, it emerges that the core of Mark's scene, temptation by Satan, not only has a verbal link with 1 Corinthians but has a link that is unique in the entire Bible.

POWER, TEACHING, HIDING AND REVEALING (1 COR 2 AND MARK 1:21–28)

In this larger section, comprising of 1 Cor 2, Paul states that when he first came to Corinth all he did was proclaim the crucified Christ. He did not speak with plausible words or wisdom but came in weakness and trembling. Paul states that he did this so that the Corinthians' faith would not rest on human wisdom but on the power of God. Paul moves on to discuss the true wisdom of God which is secret and hidden except from spiritually discerning people. Paul says that these things have been revealed to the Corinthians, because they have received the spirit of God and, therefore, they truly understand God's wisdom. Unspiritual people cannot comprehend these things.

In Mark 1:21–28 Jesus and his disciples go to Capernaum and into the synagogue. As Jesus teaches, a man with an unclean spirit cries out and Jesus performs an exorcism causing amazement in the onlookers. Following this, Jesus' fame begins to spread.

Initial General Comparison

In comparing these two sections many thematic similarities become apparent such as power, teaching and the themes of hiding and revealing. In Paul these themes occur while he is furthering his theological discussion and in Mark they occur while the narrative of Jesus' life and ministry also progresses.

Comparison and Analysis of 1 Corinthians 1–2 and Mark 1:1–28

Both texts can be divided into three subsections. In 1 Cor 2, 1 Cor 2:1–5 forms the first section and deals with Paul's description of his preaching. The second section is 1 Cor 2:6–9 and deal with God's mystery and doomed rulers while the third section is 1 Cor 2:10–16 and deals with the Spirit's scrutiny for understanding.[54] Similarly, Mark 1:21–28 can also be divided into three sections. The first is Mark 1:21–22 where Jesus is described as teaching with authority, unlike the scribes. The second section is Mark 1:23–26 where Jesus performs an exorcism and commands the unclean spirit to silence. The third and final section is 1:27–28 where people seek understanding about what has just happened and Jesus' fame begins to spread.

Literary Aspects of Mark 1:21–28

Parallels with Other Texts

Old Testament

Exorcism is not rare in the New Testament but curiously does not appear in the Old Testament. However, there is a possible connection to 2 Kgs 4:9 where Elisha is described as being ἄνθρωπος τοῦ θεοῦ ἅγιος, which is strikingly similar to what the demoniac calls Jesus in Mark 1:24, namely ὁ ἅγιος τοῦ θεοῦ. The exorcism scene in Mark 1:21–28 (as well as other Markan exorcisms), shares many elements with the scene at Carmel in 1 Kgs 18:20–40. Both involve a repeated emphasis on gathering together (συναγωγή in Mark 1:21, 23 and ἐπισυνάγω and προσάγω in 1 Kgs 18:20–21, 30), the Baal worshippers act in a demonic manner and scream with φωνῇ μεγάλῃ (1 Kgs 18:27). The demoniac does this in Mark 1:26. A key issue in both is knowing or recognizing the holy one of God (1 Kgs 18:36–39; Mark 1:24). There is a general affinity between these two texts and Mark may be evoking this here.

Egyptian Magical Papyri

J. M. Hull has argued that exorcisms and miracles belong to the category of magic.[55] Hull has identified many similarities between miracle and

---

54. Thistleton, *First Epistle*, vii.
55. Hull, *Hellenistic Magic*.

magic, particularly in exorcism.[56] The admission of the unclean spirit that he knows the identity of Jesus (v24) is similar to demonic admissions found in magical formulae from the magical papyri. For example, in one instance a demon cries out "I know you Hermes" (PGM VIII).[57] However, the papyri were written some three centuries later than Mark so the direction of influence would be here coming from Mark, if indeed there is influence.

Detailed Comparison

Context

These two sections are also the closing sections of the portions of the texts being analyzed and are the result of a certain amount of build up in each. In both instances, each section comes after a call. In 1 Cor 1:26–31 Paul reminds the Corinthians of their call while in Mark 1:16–20 Jesus calls the first of his disciples. There was a contrast between these calls; the vulnerability of the Corinthians called "according to the flesh," on the one hand, and the strength of Jesus' call with a word on the other. Both form a climax within their sub-units and draw in many of the same themes.

Theme

In these two texts there are some of the most intriguing parallels found yet in this investigation. As has already been noted, both can be divided into three subsections and each section of 1 Cor 2 corresponds, in some way, with Mark 1:21–28.

The first sub-section of both deal with preaching. Paul describes himself as preaching ". . . not in lofty words of wisdom," but with spirit and power. Jesus, on the other hand teaches not as the scribes but with great authority in a stark contrast to Paul. Moving into the second sub-section, both deal with mysteries. Paul speaks of God's wisdom which is secret and hidden—a mystery. In Mark, there is also a mystery, namely the mystery of Jesus' identity as the ". . . Holy One of God." This motif is part of the messianic secret which runs throughout the gospel.[58] Also, the rulers of this age are doomed to perish in 1 Corinthians while in Mark the unclean

---

56. Ibid., 61–72.
57. Ibid., 67.
58. See Wrede, *Messianic Secret,* and Fenton, "Mark and Paul," 89–112.

Comparison and Analysis of 1 Corinthians 1–2 and Mark 1:1–28

spirit is doomed to be exorcised by Jesus. Finally, in the third sub-section, there is a quest for understanding. Paul speaks of understanding "... the gifts bestowed," while in Mark, people try to understand what they have just seen. Both share a three part structure based around common themes.

The theme of teaching is also important to both texts. In 1 Cor 2:13 Paul discusses being taught about the wisdom of God by the spirit and not by human wisdom. In Mark 1:21 Jesus enters the synagogue at Capernaum to teach before he is interrupted by the man with the unclean spirit.

First Corinthians 2	Mark 1:21–28
Preaching not like the wise but with spirit and power (2:1–5)	Preaching with authority, not like the scribes (1:21–22)
Doomed rulers and God's mystery (2:6–9)	Doomed spirit(s) and the mystery of Jesus' identity (1:23–26)
Understanding spiritual gifts (2:10–16)	Spirit related search for understanding (1:27–28)

Action/Plot and Order

In terms of action/plot and order there are similarities that can be observed. In both, the action begins with a shift in physical location. Paul recalls going to Corinth while in Mark the narrative moves to the synagogue at Capernaum. Following this come many shared themes which all occur in the same order as indicated by their shared three-part structure.

Vocabulary

Throughout these two sections there is some share vocabulary. The use of the shared verb οἶδα is noteworthy here. First Corinthians 2:2 reads: οὐ γὰρ ἔκρινά τι εἰδέναι ἐν ὑμῖν εἰ μὴ Ἰησοῦν Χριστὸν καὶ τοῦτον ἐσταυρωμένον. Paul has decided to know nothing apart from Jesus. In Mark, Jesus is also the one who is known, only this time by the demoniac. Mark 1:24 reads: λέγων· Τί ἡμῖν καὶ σοί, Ἰησοῦ Ναζαρηνέ; ἦλθες ἀπολέσαι ἡμᾶς; οἶδά σε τίς εἶ, ὁ ἅγιος τοῦ θεοῦ. Both contain multiple uses of teaching related words such as διδαχή, διδακτός, and διδάσκω. Other shared words are ἔρχομαι, πνεῦμα, ἄνθρωπος, and ἔχω.

Completeness

All the major elements of 1 Cor 2 find some similarity with Mark 1:21–28, including the mirroring thematic changes within the context of a three part internal division within a single unit of text.

Assessment and Conclusion

In assessing the data collected, some of the most intriguing similarities thus far come to light which can be summarized as follows:

- Both sections share a three part structure.
- Both share themes of preaching, teaching, hiding and revealing and a quest for understanding.
- Both shared common words.

Mark's basic narrative of Jesus' ministry appears to follow closely Paul's theological letter in 1 Cor 2. Added to this are the elements incorporated from 1 and 2 Kings. These affinities go beyond mere coincidence and 1 Cor 2 needs to be considered as a source for Mark 1:21–28 and as part of Mark's textual weaving.

ASSESSING THE EVIDENCE: THE CRITERIA FOR JUDGING LITERARY DEPENDENCE

It is here that the full importance of the criteria for judging literary dependence will become apparent. It will allow the various data that has been collected to be gathered together in order to properly assess whether or not a case for literary dependence can be made.

External Criteria

1. Date—Date is not an issue here with regards to Mark and 1 Corinthians in the context of Markan priority. First Corinthians and the Gospel of Mark were written roughly fifteen years apart thus allowing time for the letter to circulate
2. Accessibility—Paul's letters were undoubtedly quickly distributed. Even within the New Testament, Paul's letters are mentioned in 2 Pet 3:15–16

and he is discussed and quoted by many early church fathers[59] Paul's letters must have been readily available and distributed for them to have made such an important impact in the development of early Christianity.

Distance appears not to have been a problem for early Christians and people within the Greco-Roman world at large. People were ready and willing to make the long journeys between cities.[60] Therefore it is entirely plausible that Mark could have known and have had access to the letters of Paul, including 1 Corinthians.

The idea of an epistle travelling long distances is not problematic as Paul composed his letters far away from their intended destination. Romans, for example, is held to have been written in Corinth.[61] Documents did travel great distances, allowing people to have access to them.

3. Status of the text—The issue of the status of the text is related to the above issue of availability. A text that was readily available and distributed was more likely to be known. That Paul was known by other New Testament writers is evident in 2 Peter and Acts and he was used by the early church fathers. Also, the fact that so many of Paul's letters were included in the canon of the New Testament shows the high regard in which he and his letters were held.

4. Outside uses of the source text—First Corinthians was used by the early church fathers, as already stated and was likely to have been known by the author of 2 Peter.

Internal Criteria

1. Similarities of context, theme, action/plot, order and completeness—While progressing through 1 Cor 1 and 2 and Mark 1:1–28 many similarities of context theme, action/plot, order and completeness were noted. While there is no need for repetition of every parallel here a recapitulation of the most important will be useful.

   Context—In terms of the overall context of these two sections both come at the start of each respective document and both form roughly the first half of a larger unit of text. However, all texts have a beginning and this cannot contribute to a case for literary dependence.

---

59. See, Clement, *1 Clem.* 5:2, 6–7; 47:1–5; Ignatius, *Eph.* 12:1–2; Ignatius, *Rom.* 4:3; Polycarp, *Phil.* 2:3; 9:1; and 11:3. These are only a few examples of the many available.

60. Thompson, "The Holy Internet," 49–70.

61. Fitzmyer, "Letter to the Romans," 291.

The Quest for Mark's Sources

Theme—Thematically 1 Cor 1–2 and Mark 1:1–28 share much. Both focus on the themes of higher powers, baptism, the religious call, preaching, unity, faith and revelation amongst others. Each section compared had a thematic link with the corresponding section. Even when vocabulary links were limited, a distinct thematic link was always present. Often a contrasting view on a particular theme was present. For example, in relation to the theme of unity in 1 Cor 1:10–13 and Mark 1:16–20, Paul presents a scene of disunity and division in relation to following Christ while Mark presents a scene of harmonious unity. This contrast was seen with many themes and always Mark presents an ideal in contrast to problems in 1 Corinthians. This contrast could be deliberate on Mark's part and serves a pedagogical purpose in presenting what Christians should do—something which they are not doing in Corinth.

Action/Plot—In terms of action/plot the differing genres make finding similarities in this area unlikely. However, there were certain similarities of note. Both began with an appeal to a higher power. It was shown that Mark is alone amongst the gospels in sharing this similarity with 1 Corinthians and other Pauline letters. Again contrasting elements were found. While 1 Corinthians looks forward to a future revelation of the blameless, Mark looks back to a revelation of the beloved. The plot points create a contrast to what is presented in 1 Corinthians. This is seen again with baptism where Paul baptizes few and John many. Aspects of Mark's plot present parallels and instructive contrasts with elements of 1 Corinthians. This, of course, overlaps somewhat with the shared themes.

Order—On a large scale 1 Cor 1–2 matches Mark 1:1–28 when divided into sections. The order is rough with a few sections of Mark 1:1–28 not following the same order as 1 Cor 1–2. This is easily explainable because of the differing genres and Mark's reliance on other sources. On a smaller scale there were elements of shared order within the compared sections. The most striking of these was in comparing 1 Cor 2 with Mark 1:21–28 where a three part structure based around shared themes was found in the same order.

Completeness—Is every major aspect of 1 Cor 1–2 matched in some way within Mark 1:1–28. On a larger level most aspects are represented. The broad themes of 1 Cor 1–2 including unity, baptism and the religious call are found in Mark 1:1–28. However, there are parts of 1 Cor 1–2 that do not find a parallel in Mark 1:1–28. For example, the explicit discussion of the cross in these opening chapters is not represented in Mark 1:1–28. However, this is largely intelligible. Mark is writing a narrative

Comparison and Analysis of 1 Corinthians 1–2 and Mark 1:1–28

and it is simply too soon in the gospel to introduce the cross. Paul is not restricted by the constraints of narrative.

2. Common Vocabulary—As was seen through the analysis of the two texts there was a lot of shared vocabulary. However, much of the vocabulary is not distinctive to Mark and Paul. This does not necessarily mean that it is not significant. While the vocabulary may not be unique, and can be found elsewhere, it should be considered along with all the other similarities noted. The vocabulary forms part of a series of links which makes it significant. For example, it was seen how 1 Cor 1:1–3 and Mark 1:1–3 share a group of six common words including Χριστός, Ἰησοῦς, θεός, which are some of the most common words in the New Testament. However, it was also shown that it is only in Mark and the epistles that these words are found grouped together at the very start of a text. Other gospels do not do this. It is unique to Mark and Paul and in general indicates the possible influence of Paul's epistles on Mark. Therefore, in certain instances while the vocabulary may not be significant, its placement it. There is, however, some significant shared vocabulary that needs to be mentioned.

The use of the rare verb καταρτίζω is somewhat puzzling as, although it is rare, the usages in 1 Cor 1:10 and Mark 1:19 are different. Paul is asking the Corinthians to unite and mend themselves while in Mark the brothers James and John are mending their fishing nets. In terms of pedagogy, Mark may be providing an example of followers of Jesus who do not need to be mended. They are mending the nets for the fish and will now become fishers of people. The mending of nets keeps the fish together, just as Paul wishes to keep the Corinthians together.

Also, both use a similar phrase in 1 Cor 1:8 and Mark 1:9. Paul uses the phrase ἐν τῇ ἡμέρᾳ. Mark uses a similar phrase ἐν ἐκείναις ταῖς ἡμέραις (v9), variations of which can be found throughout the LXX.

However, vocabulary is not the final arbitrator in determining the issue of dependence, although it obviously helps. For example, the affinities between 1 Cor 2 and Mark 1:21–28 are stronger than in other sections as they share many themes, action and order yet the amount of shared vocabulary is quite limited.

3. Literary convention(s) being employed—level of text absorption—What has been seen, as a by-product of the explorations into Mark and 1 Corinthians, is a strong dependence on the Old Testament and in particular 1 and 2 Kings. Mark may have woven together parts of 1 Corinthians

with 1 Kings in the creation of something new. This process is known as *contaminatio* and pervades all ancient literature.

One of the main literary techniques being used by Mark here is one of reversal. Again and again it is seen in Mark 1:1–28 that elements of 1 Cor 1–2 may have been used and turned on their head. This is something which the author of Mark appears to employ throughout his gospel and is even personified by the character of Jesus who is the antithesis of the expected messiah. Mark takes what is expected and turns it on itself. This permeates down to how the writer uses some of his sources. The contrast involves the processes of positivization and negativization which both reverse aspects of the source text or texts.

Also seen are possible uses of distribution and distillation. Vocabulary from certain sections of 1 Cor 1–2 is found scattered throughout Mark 1:1–28 and certain themes are distilled to one or two hook words.

In terms of the level of text absorption seen here, it is difficult to determine, as it does not appear to fit into any one category already established. What is seen is consistent with elements of allusion and, in particular, transforming allusion. Mark certainly does not conform to the situation in Corinth and often presents contrasts to the Corinthian situation and, therefore, transforms it. There are also similarities to Hays' imitation categories. Mark's weaving together of multiple sources is consistent with eclectic imitation where not one source is given primary significance but rather multiple sources are mingled together. Mark uses many Old Testament texts in the composition of his narrative and even has affinities with certain intertestamental and classical texts. The similarities seen with 1 Cor 1–2 were not as strong as with Old Testament texts and this is consistent with eclectic imitation.

There is also the possibility of dialectical imitation where a contrast is formed with the source text within its new literary context. The contrast between Mark and 1 Corinthians seems to indicate this possibility as the texts do appear to be complementary to each other.

4. Intelligibility/Interpretability of the differences—In spite of multiple similarities between 1 Cor 1–2 and Mark 1:1–28 there are obvious differences. If differences were looked for in the same manner as similarities, many would be found. Are these differences problematic? Or do they, perhaps, indicate that there is no relationship between these two texts?

   Firstly, the role played by the difference in genre needs to be recognized. Paul is writing a letter and is concerned with a particular situation in Corinth and is constructing theological arguments. He is not concerned with plot or story as Mark is. Therefore, Mark has to appeal to other sources such as 1 and 2 Kings for material. An example of the differences brought about by genre would be the apparent lack of use, in Mark 1:1–28, of the explicit references to the crucifixion found in 1 Cor 1:18–25. A source dealing explicitly with the crucifixion simply has no place in Mark 1:1–28 and is, therefore, not used here. For Paul, who is not writing a narrative, the cross can be discussed anywhere.

While interpreting the differences, the role played by multiple sources should be recognized. First Corinthians may be only one of many sources and will not always be used by Mark at every point. At the core of Mark's gospel is the basic story of the life of Jesus which existed before Mark's gospel and which must ultimately be the driving force behind the entire gospel. First Corinthians is only one component of a larger web of allusions.

Probing Criteria

1. Strong and weak connections—In comparison and analysis of 1 Cor 1–2 and Mark 1:1–28 many similarities were noted. However, many of these connections were weak and may not indicate any literary connection. Many texts share elements and this is to be expected, however, this does not point to a literary relationship. Yet, each individual weak connection should not be viewed in isolation. Weak links are only part of the debate and they need to be viewed as part of a larger chain of similarities and as part of Mark's larger textual weaving. On their own, certain affinities do not hold but as supporting evidence they become significant. However, they only become significant and can only be used as supporting evidence if there are strong connections which indicate a literary relationship.

   In weighing the strong similarities against the weak based on vocabulary alone, no significantly strong connections could be made to elevate the weak connections to supporting evidence. However, as has been consistently demonstrated, there were many thematic similarities, some more apparent than others. While a few themes on their own mean little, they were observed throughout both texts and in every section analyzed. A tipping point is reached where this can no longer be ignored or pushed to one side and dismissed.

2. Similarities that may be due to a common tradition—The possibility of a common tradition that explains the similarities between Mark and Paul has often been proposed but remains troublesome as it ventures into the

realm of hypothetical texts. However, it is a possibility that cannot be fully excluded without due consideration. Yet, as has been demonstrated, Mark skillfully weaves together strands from many sources, one of which may be 1 Corinthians. Given Mark's careful use of literary sources, a common tradition appears to be the less likely scenario.

3. Similarities that may be due to a general familiarity of the source text—Can the similarities noted be ascribed to a general familiarity of 1 Corinthians by the author of Mark? This notion is a possibility but would be more applicable to similarities in theology which was not the focus in the above chapter. While many similarities were noted in terms of theme and action/plot a general familiarity of 1 Corinthians would likely produce theological similarities. These have been noted by many other commentators, many of whom have concluded that Mark was working within a Pauline sphere of influence. The similarities noted here do not fit into this hypothesis.

4. Redundancy—Does another source or sources render all the connections to 1 Cor 1–2 redundant? While Mark is heavily reliant upon the Old Testament and 1 and 2 Kings in particular, this does not preclude dependence on other texts. Neither does it preclude the possibility of Mark having minor sources. However, while Old Testament sources do account for much of the material in Mark 1:1–28 they do not overlap entirely with the connections noted with 1 Cor 1–2. While one source may be more important to Mark, another may also have been woven into the fabric of the narrative.

CONCLUSION

Now that 1 Cor 1–2 and Mark 1:1–28 have been compared and analyzed and all the collected data has been looked at through the criteria for judging literary dependence, what can be said about the relationship between the two texts?

The data presents some interesting possibilities. What has become apparent is that Mark worked with a plethora of written sources, particularly from the Old Testament. First and Second Kings, along with Isaiah, emerge as major sources. Two or more can be evoked in one place and there were many parallels with classical literature as noted. However, none of these sources accounted entirely for certain data which had similarities with 1 Corinthians.

Comparison and Analysis of 1 Corinthians 1–2 and Mark 1:1–28

While Mark is reliant on Old Testament texts there is also the underlying story of Jesus of Nazareth to be taken into account. Whatever its nature it, along with Old Testament texts, forms the base for Mark 1:1–28. In terms of the similarities noted, some were stronger than others with many weak similarities being found. The vocabulary links were unconvincing with many common words found and these make only a small contribution in a case for literary dependence. There were also common words tied to shared themes. Two pieces of vocabulary should be mentioned. The first is the similar phrasing found in 1 Cor 1:8 and Mark 1:9. This appears striking when considered alongside the thematic links within the two sections but when considered against the larger use of similar phrases throughout the LXX and New Testament, any significance becomes diminished. Another important similarity is the common usage of the verb καταρτίζω because of its uncommon nature.

As was seen throughout the analysis, there were also many affinities of action/plot, order and completeness. However, it was thematically that the most parallels were seen. From the beginning to the end the texts showed common themes such as higher powers, baptism, revelation, unity, displays of power, teaching, and the spiritual call. Around this was some shared vocabulary. These themes permeated the plot in Mark. Interestingly, Mark often reads as a contrast to the situation in Corinth. If this is deliberate then Mark is positivizing the situation in Corinth. The purpose of this could be pedagogical in nature. Mark is possibly showing how Christians should act, rather than how they are acting.

When all the data is considered together a certain ambiguity is left. Many similarities were found and the majority of these were weak in nature. However, it is together that they need to be viewed. Not only this, they need to be viewed against Mark's major sources and narrative purpose. The possibility that 1 Corinthians is a lesser source for Mark is a real one that requires further investigation. The similarities seen here show some consistency with transforming allusion, eclectic imitation, and possibly dialectical imitation. However, this remains to be seen and further investigation into other portions of the texts is required.

— 6 —

Comparison and Analysis of 1 Corinthians 5 and Mark 6:14–29

INTRODUCTION

FIRST CORINTHIANS 5:1–13 AND Mark 6:14–29 have been selected for analysis because of their shared subject matter. First Corinthians 5:1–13 involves a man living with his father's wife while Mark 6:14–29 involves a man living with his brother's wife. The two also form their own literary units within their larger texts. First Corinthians 5:1–13 is generally held together as one literary unit as is Mark 6:14–29.[1] These two texts come from the central sections of their respective documents and both come near the beginning of a shift in each text as well. First Corinthians 5 forms part of a sub-unit consisting of chapters 5 and 6 and deals with infighting and moral failings in the Corinthian church.[2] Mark 6:14–29 forms the beginning of a

---

1. For 1 Cor 5 see Fitzmyer, *First Corinthians*, 228–47. Conzelmann, *1 Corinthians*, 194–202. Ciampa and Rosner, *First Corinthians*, 196–221. Ciampa and Rosner, while recognizing the unit of 1 Cor 5, divide the chapter into 5 rough sections which are as follows: a. Removing the immoral man (1 Cor 5:1–2); b. Paul stands behind expulsion (1 Cor 5:3–5); c. The metaphor of years (1 Cor 5:6–8); d. Separating from the immoral man (1 Cor 5:9–11); e. Expel the wicked person (1 Cor 5:12–13). For Mark see Marcus, *Mark*, 1:394–404. Hooker, *Gospel*, 157–62.

2. Conzelmann, *1 Corinthians*, vi–viii. Orr and Walther, *1 Corinthians*, x–xv. Murphy-O'Connor, "First Letter to the Corinthians," 798–815.

section which begins at 6:6 and runs on to 8:21 and loosely revolves around the theme of food.[3]

DETAILED ANALYSIS

In 1 Cor 5 Paul begins a new theological thread in his letter by tackling the issue of sexual immorality among the Corinthian church. It has been reported to Paul that a man has been living with his father's wife and this type of immorality is not found "even among the pagans." Paul argues that this man should be handed over to Satan in order that he may be saved. He urges the Corinthians not to associate with this person and not to eat with him.

In Mark 6:14–29 the death of John the Baptist is narrated. The section opens with Herod learning of Jesus' miracles and he assumes that John has returned whom he has beheaded. The beheading is then narrated through flashback. Herod, who has been living with his brother's wife, is berated by John for this. Herodias then holds a grudge against him and instructs her daughter, when Herod offers her anything she wants, to ask for the head of John the Baptist. Herod reluctantly agrees. John's disciples come and remove his body for burial.

Initial General Comparison

Upon first glance at the texts, the most obvious similarity concerns the morality of a man living with, or marrying, the wife of a relative. In 1 Corinthians a man is said to be living with his father's wife (presumably not the man's own mother) and in Mark, Herod has married his brother's wife. The actions of both people are condemned. The background to both scenes is a meal setting. Paul warns the Corinthians not to eat with the sexually immoral person while in Mark it is the sexually immoral person who is hosting a banquet.

There are, however, some obvious differences that need to be mentioned. Paul's discussion is part of a longer discussion concerning a variety of sins being committed in the Corinthian church while in Mark the main thrust of the episode is the death of John the Baptist. Paul lists certain sins while this section in Mark contains no such listing.

---

3. Williamson, *Mark*, vii–ix. Marcus, *Mark*, 1:vi–vii.

The Quest for Mark's Sources
Literary Aspects of Mark 6:14–29

Parallels with Other Texts

Old Testament

The obvious background to this section is the law in the book of Leviticus which prohibits a man from having sexual intercourse with his brother's wife, ἀσχημοσύνην γυναικὸς ἀδελφοῦ σου οὐκ ἀποκαλύψεις· ἀσχημοσύνη ἀδελφοῦ σού ἐστιν (Lev 18:16). This is further iterated in the same text, ὃς ἂν λάβῃ τὴν γυναῖκα τοῦ ἀδελφοῦ αὐτοῦ, ἀκαθαρσία ἐστίν· ἀσχημοσύνην τοῦ ἀδελφοῦ αὐτοῦ ἀπεκάλυψεν, ἄτεκνοι ἀποθανοῦνται (Lev 20:21).

There is, however, a loophole to this law which states when a man's brother has died childless he can take his brother's wife as his own.

> Ἐὰν δὲ κατοικῶσιν ἀδελφοὶ ἐπὶ τὸ αὐτὸ καὶ ἀποθάνῃ εἷς ἐξ αὐτῶν, σπέρμα δὲ μὴ ᾖ αὐτῷ, οὐκ ἔσται ἡ γυνὴ τοῦ τεθνηκότος ἔξω ἀνδρὶ μὴ ἐγγίζοντι· ὁ ἀδελφὸς τοῦ ἀνδρὸς αὐτῆς εἰσελεύσεται πρὸς αὐτὴν καὶ λήμψεται αὐτὴν ἑαυτῷ γυναῖκα καὶ συνοικήσει αὐτῇ. (Deut 25:5)

This, however, is not the context of Herod's marriage to Herodias as Herod's brother was still alive and not childless.[4]

Although it is Jesus who is compared to Elijah here, it is John who appears to be more like Elijah. Just as John is cast as Elijah at the opening of Mark's gospel, so he is again at this point. Like Elijah, John shows a zeal for the Lord and his law and is not afraid to confront a king and face his wrath for this.[5] Elijah also antagonizes a king's wife who seeks his death (1 Kgs 19:2). The portrayal of Herodias as a Jezebel-like character creates a dark scene and a connection to 1 Kings that is hard to miss.

The most striking similarity to this story comes from the book of Esther. When 'beautiful young virgins' are sought for King Ahasuerus the

---

4. Mark's text is full of inaccuracies concerning Herod's family tree. Herodias was not Philip's wife but rather the wife of another half-brother also called Herod. The daughter mentioned in Mark is likely to be Herod Antipas' niece from his brother's marriage. This daughter, called Herodias in Mark's text, is also known as Salome. Mark's inaccuracies are understandable considering the amount of inbreeding within the Herodian dynasty coupled with many siblings having the same name. Marcus has provided a simplified Herodian family tree, relevant to this story which provides clarity. Marcus, *Mark*, 1:394. Collins also provides a good breakdown of the family relationships at this time. Collins, *Mark*, 301–306. Another inaccuracy is that Herod is called a king when he was actually a Roman tetrarch. The use of king may reflect popular usage at the time. Collins, *Mark*, 303.

5. Marcus, *Mark*, 1:400. See 1 Kgs 19:10 and 1 Kgs 21:17–24.

young Jewish Esther is described as pleasing to him (καὶ ἤρεσεν αὐτῷ τὸ κοράσιον—Esth 2:9). Later in the story, once she has become his Queen, he gives her a request and promises her up to half his kingdom. Herod's offer to his daughter is strikingly similar when compared to Esther and both contain the phrases εἶπεν ὁ βασιλεὺς and ἡμίσους τῆς βασιλείας μου. The verbal similarities are striking and this passage from Esther provides a huge source for Mark at this point. The proximity of a banquet scene only serves to strengthen this connection.

Apocrypha

The apocryphal book of Judith provides further similarities to the death of John the Baptist in Mark. Judith, like Herodias, uses her femininity to charm a man. She dresses "in all her woman's finery" much to the delight of Holofernes who believes he is being successful in seducing Judith. Judith is described as having pleased Holofernes, although a different verb is used to express this in both Judith and Mark. Judith later beheads a drunk Holofernes in his tent and the head is placed in a food bag. John's head, in Mark, is placed on a platter. Both are connected with food and both beheadings, like the request in Esther, take place around the events of a banquet.[6]

Qumran

The Damascus Document prohibits the marriage to a niece which is exactly what Herod Antipas had done.[7]

Classical Texts

The motif of a king being forced to grant a request at a banquet is one that runs throughout classical literature. Herodotus tells a story of the Persian king Xerxes offering Artaynte anything she wanted. She chooses a mantle that Xerxes was wearing that was made by his wife, Amestris. Xerxes didn't want to part with the mantle and offered Artaynte gold and cities but she refused. Amestris saw Artaynte wearing the mantle and sought revenge.

---

6. See Jdt 12:10—13:9.
7. CD 5:8–11.

However, Xerxes was in love with Artaynte's mother who was his brother's wife. Amestris, therefore, seeks revenge against the mother of Artaynte and waits for the banquet of the king's birthday to ask for the woman to be handed over to her. Herodotus reports that on a king's birthday, all requests must be answered according to Persian custom. His brother's wife is handed over and her breasts, nose, ears, lips and tongue are fed to the dogs.[8] The parallels between this story and the death of John the Baptist are startling. Both revolve around the desire for a brother's wife, requests being granted at banquets and the occasion of a king's birthday.

Livy also reports a similar story about a man named Flamininus who was in love with a courtesan. At a banquet Flamininus boasts about all the men he has imprisoned ready to behead. The courtesan requests to view a beheading and a prisoner is then beheaded at the banquet for her entertainment.[9]

Two post-Markan stories deserve note. Firstly Plutarch, in his life of Crassus, describes how the decapitated head of Crassus is brought to a banquet for all to see.[10] Secondly, Josephus reports a story about the nephew of Herod Antipas, Agrippa, who holds a lavish banquet for the emperor Caligula who is so impressed that he offers Agrippa a request. Agrippa asks Caligula to do away with his plans to erect a statue of himself in the Jerusalem temple. Caligula, bound by the offer of a request, agrees.[11]

While these latter two stories cannot be considered sources for Mark, they do, along with the earlier stories mentioned, show the prevalence of the ancient custom of rulers granting requests on significant days, particularly birthdays. Requests are often violent in nature. There is also a common connection between eating, something which sustains life, and a violent act which ends life.

Mark 6:14–29—An interpolation?

Unlike the other texts being analyzed in Mark, no other has so many question marks concerning its authenticity than Mark 6:14–29. This is the only substantial story in the Gospel of Mark that does not deal directly with Jesus and his actions. This has led some scholars to conclude that his

---

8. Herodotus, *Hist.* 9.108–13.
9. Livy, *Hist. Rom.* 39–43.
10. Plutarch, *Crass.*, 33.1–3.
11. Marcus, *Mark*, 1:400, Josephus, *Ant.* 18.289–304.

Comparison and Analysis of 1 Corinthians 5 and Mark 6:14–29

story is, therefore, traditional material that Mark has inherited and placed, somewhat haphazardly, into his narrative. Frank Kermode called this story a "heterodiegetic analepsis," which is a flashback belonging to a different story, here being the story of John the Baptist. The main reason Kermode gives to attributing this to another story is that it does not further the main narrative of the gospel.[12] Theissen argued that this story is a court legend while Marcus called it "folkloristic."[13] Supporting the hypothesis that it is traditional material is the sudden change in grammatical style throughout this section. The common historical present tense used throughout Mark, disappears at this point and is replaced by the aorist and imperfect tenses.[14] However, this change in grammatical style seems perfectly plausible and understandable as Mark is looking back to a past event where the historical present would not be appropriate. While the entire gospel is narrating past events, this is a past event within the framework of the narrative story making a change in tense both warranted and necessary.

These are, however, many aspects of the text that point to the meticulous crafting of this scene that show its placement to be completely deliberate. Its placement fills in the gap between the sending out of the twelve by Jesus and their return.

Jesus' fate is also foreshadowed. The whole story indicates that missionary activity will result in a violent death. As John was Jesus' forerunner the reader can, therefore, expect Jesus to suffer a similar fate.[15] However, there is an element of false foreshadowing in that John's disciples come to claim his body for burial while Jesus' disciples will scatter, leaving Jesus to be buried by Joseph of Arimathea; a stranger.[16]

Marcus has illustrated that this story is part of a larger subtext surrounding the behavior of women. Close to this story on either side is the story of the haemorrhaging woman (5:24–34) and the Syrophoenician woman (7:24–30). Both of these stories revolve around women of great faith who are not afraid to seek out Jesus and are rewarded for this action. The two women involved in the death of John the Baptist are the antithesis of these faithful women and act in a macabre and almost demonic fashion. Therefore, the two faithful women provide a frame around the two evil

12. Kermode, *Genesis of Secrecy*, 128–31.
13. Theissen, *Gospels in Context*, 81. Marcus, *Mark*, 1:402.
14. Marcus, *Mark*, 1:297–98.
15. Ibid.
16. Collins, *Mark*, 314.

women.[17] Given the common usage of literary sandwiches in the Gospel of Mark, this seems entirely possible. Added to this portrayal of almost demonic women is the portrayal of Herod himself. He appears as a demonic caricature who fears the "holy" John but yet seems interested by him, keeping him close.[18] The Gerasene demonic also fears Jesus and refers to him as being holy and rushes to Jesus when he sees him. This demonic picture of the Herodian banquet is finished with the presentation of the head of John the Baptist on a platter which almost converts the scene into a demonic Eucharist.[19] This story is positioned carefully and has been meticulously crafted and woven into the fabric of the narrative.

Detailed Comparison

Context

Both texts come close to the beginning of new literary units within their larger documents. Paul is beginning his discussion of sexual immorality which will lead to a discussion of marriage and divorce while the narrative in Mark comes close to the beginning of a new section which starts at 6:6 and deals with mass feedings and the various conflicts with Jewish groups that Jesus encounters. Both larger sections in these documents are generally concerned with morality and behavior.

Theme

Thematically these two sections are similar. At the core of both is the theme of sexual immorality. Paul is dealing with a man who is living with his father's wife while the narrative in Mark describes Herod Antipas living with his brother's wife.[20] In both texts the living situation of both men is condemned. The theme of food is introduced into both texts at this point and this theme will carry on into chapter 11 in 1 Corinthians and to the end of chapter 8 in Mark. The use of the food theme is similar in both also. In 1 Corinthians Paul warns against eating with the sexually immoral person

---

17. Marcus, *Mark*, 1:403.
18. Ibid., 1:401.
19. Ibid., 1:403.
20. The law behind Paul's offence is Lev 18:7–8 which is in the same section that prohibits sexual intercourse with a brother's wife.

Comparison and Analysis of 1 Corinthians 5 and Mark 6:14-29

in the Corinthian church while in Mark the sexually immoral person is the host of a banquet. There is a certain contrast in this theme in that, while in 1 Corinthians, Paul is urging people to disassociate and not eat with the offending person, in Mark the offending person is the cause of people coming together to eat in the "demonic Eucharist." This contrast is furthered with the theme of the destruction of the body. Paul says that this person should be handed over to Satan for the destruction of their flesh while in Mark, John, who is judging like Paul, is the victim of the destruction of the body. Herodias, the cause of this destruction, can be said to be a satanic character and the wrong person is ultimately the victim in contradiction to 1 Corinthians. This pattern of sharply contrasting elements continues from that already observed in 1 Cor 1-2 and Mark 1:1-28.

Another thematic link comes in the form of Paul's mention of pagans. Paul claims that this type of immorality is not found even among the pagans, which implies that pagans have a lower moral standard than early Christians. In Mark, Herod is celebrating his birthday which was something frowned upon in both Judaism and Christianity where birthdays were not observed and was considered to be idolatrous, pagan behavior.[21]

Action/Plot and Order

The strongest parallels between these two sections come in terms of the action, plot and order as a chain of similarities occur in a similar sequence. Both are dealing with a sexually immoral person, one is living with his father's wife while the other is married to his brother's wife. This action in both is then condemned. In 1 Corinthians the person condemning this action, Paul, calls for the removal of that person while in Mark it is the person who is condemning, John, who is removed. Paul calls for people not to eat with this person while in Mark it is the offending person who is bringing people together to eat. Finally, Paul calls for this person to be handed over to Satan for the destruction of their flesh while in Mark, John is killed by a satanic character. This occurs in the same order in both texts.

---

21. Marcus, *Mark*, 1:395.

Vocabulary

In terms of vocabulary there are many shared words such as ἔχω, γυνή, αἴρω, ὄνομα, δύναμις, πνεῦμα, οἶδα, ἐξέρχομαι, and ἀδελφός. All of the words shared between the two texts are very common in the New Testament and are, therefore, hard to use in a case of literary dependence but there are some points that need to be mentioned. The verb ἀκούω is used in a similar fashion in both texts. It occurs multiple times in Mark but only once in 1 Corinthians. The usage in 1 Cor 5:1 and Mark 6:14 at the start of both sections are somewhat similar in that both describe a report. Paul is hearing a report about the sexual immorality within the Corinthian church while in Mark, Herod hears about the activity of Jesus. Both texts also use δύναμις to discuss the power of Jesus.

Completeness

In looking for completeness the question has to be asked whether or not every aspect of 1 Cor 5:1–13 is matched, in some way, by part of Mark 6:14–29? Most of this section of 1 Corinthians is matched by the story of the death of John the Baptist. Sexual immorality, a man living with someone he should not be, the removal of a person, Satan, destruction of the body and the theme of eating are all present in both texts. The parable-like language of 1 Cor 5:6–8 is not matched here by Mark and neither is the list of sins that Paul gives. However, there are such sections within Mark in other places.

Assessment and Conclusion

In conclusion, what can be said about the relationship between 1 Cor 5:1–13 and Mark 6:14–29? The two share many details that appear to go beyond the level of coincidence. The main similarities are as follows:

- Both texts are centered on a person who is sexually immoral and living with a person prohibited by Jewish law.
- The actions of the sexually immoral person are condemned.
- Paul calls for the removal of that person while in Mark, John is removed.
- The destruction of flesh is present in both.
- The theme of eating together is present in both.

Comparison and Analysis of 1 Corinthians 5 and Mark 6:14–29

- Satan is mentioned in 1 Cor 5:5 and satanic characters appear in Mark.
- There is a correlation of order between the two texts.

The existence of many similar scenes in classical literature indicated that this is somewhat of a type scene and a common literary device adopted from ancient cultural practice. However, this does not appear to be the case with Mark who clearly draws on the book of Esther with much shared vocabulary. The many similarities noted with 1 Cor 5 indicate some form of literary relationship as well. Mark again appears to be weaving multiple texts together.

ASSESSING THE EVIDENCE: THE CRITERIA FOR JUDGING LITERARY DEPENDENCE

External Criteria

There is no need to go through the internal criteria again as the date, accessibility, status and outside uses of the texts have already been discussed in the previous chapter. The data collected in this chapter has no bearing on this information and, therefore, does not need to be repeated.

Internal Criteria

1. Similarities of context, theme, action/plot, order and completeness.

   Context—Both sections come near the beginning of new units within their own documents. However, the surrounding texts do not match in a manner that would indicate literary dependence at this point.

   Theme—In terms of theme these two texts shared many affinities. Three strong thematic connections were found. The first was the man living with his father's/brother's wife which is the issue around which both texts are revolving. The second is condemnation and the third is food. This theme also contained a contrast in that while Paul was urging people not to eat with the offending person, in Mark it is the offending person who is the cause of people coming together to eat. Two further themes also presented themselves. The first was the destruction of the body in both, although in different ways. The final thematic link was the mention of pagans in Paul and Herod acting in a pagan way by celebrating his birthday. These latter two themes are somewhat vague in nature while the first three are more specific. A case can be made for the first three themes in terms of literary dependence but the last two themes can only contribute as supporting evidence.

Action/plot—Shared elements of action/plot are somewhat related to the common themes and are compounded by the fact that Paul is not writing in a narrative form and is, therefore, largely devoid of plot. However, there is a loose plot in 1 Cor 5:1–13 in that a man is living with his father's wife and this is causing disruption to the Corinthian community. This is reflected in Mark.

Order—The common themes, shared between the two texts, occur in the same order which deepens the connection.

Completeness—As the shared thematic links indicate there is a lot that connects these two texts and most of the major elements of 1 Cor 5:1–13 are reflected, in order, in Mark 6:14–29. However, there are elements that do not find an affinity in Mark. Firstly, the parable-like language of 1 Cor 5:6–8 finds no counterpart in Mark 6:14–29 and neither is there a list of sins as in 1 Cor 5:11. While not every aspects finds a counterpart, the majority of this section of 1 Corinthians does.

2. Common Vocabulary—The majority of the vocabulary that was found to be shared between these two texts was largely common to the New Testament. While a lot of this vocabulary was clustered around the shared thematic elements noted, none of the words were singular enough to contribute to a case for literary dependence and neither were there sufficient words found close enough together.

3. Literary convention being employed and level of absorption—The similarities noted above are consistent with many methods used in text absorption. *Varatio* is consistent with what has been observed. Details of 1 Cor 5:1–13 appear, in a varied form in Mark 6:14–29. The details about Herod, given in Mark, could be due to contemporization or a particular form of it. While contemporization is usually bringing a text up to date, Mark, writing his narrative in the past, does the opposite and puts the details of 1 Corinthians back in time to make it fit within the narrative. *Contaminatio* is also present in that Mark uses multiple sources and blends them together.

With regards to the level of text absorption being observed here, there are two basic options. Firstly, what has been observed could be conforming allusion. Mark does not really challenge the basic message of Paul's text and it is, therefore, not transforming in nature. Rather the central

Comparison and Analysis of 1 Corinthians 5 and Mark 6:14-29

message is largely the same and the connections deep enough that it can be called allusion. The second option is eclectic imitation which involves the mingling together of sources which accounts for differences being made to the source. Given the amount of Old Testament sources underlying Mark, this latter option seems to be more likely.

4. Intelligibility of the differences—However, there are differences, as mentioned. Are these intelligible? The first difference is small but deserves mention. Paul is discussing a man living with this father's wife while in Mark it is Herod who is living with his brother's wife. If 1 Cor 5:1-13 is a source for Mark here, why has Mark not kept all the detail of the father's wife? The answer is a simple historical one. Herod has married his brother's wife and, therefore, provided Mark with an actual model around which to construct his account of the death of John the Baptist. The law prohibiting this comes from the same body of laws prohibiting sexual intercourse with a father's wife. Therefore, the jump from one to the other is both small and understandable.

A second difference is the presence of parable-like language in 1 Cor 5:6-8 which is absent in this section of Mark. Mark has just finished a large section of parables and in such a tense scene that results in the gruesome death of Jesus' forerunner, a sudden digression into a parable would be out of place. Further to this, all the parables in Mark are spoken by Jesus who is absent from this scene. The list of sins that Paul mentions is also absent from Mark but a similar list is found at Mark 7:21-22.

Probing Criteria

1. Strong and weak connections—Throughout the analysis there were both strong and weak connections. The strongest connections were thematic in nature while the weakest were in terms of vocabulary. While the weak connections cannot, solely, form a case for literary dependence, they do take on significance as supporting evidence in the presence of the strong connections that were found here. These close thematic links are of sufficient detail to warrant a case for dependence. The weaker connections do not destroy this case and should not be viewed in isolation.

2. Similarities due to a common tradition—Both texts make reference to similar laws in Leviticus which lies at the root of each text. However, these laws do not account for all the data in both and the common thread of themes indicate a closer relationship than one of common tradition.

3. Similarities due to a general familiarity of text—If only weak connections were found then general familiarity could be considered a viable option. However, the similarities were found to be close in many respects which indicate that the author of Mark had more than a passing knowledge of 1 Corinthians.

4. Redundancy—Does the presence of other sources for Mark 6:14–29 make any similarities to 1 Cor 5:1–13 redundant? While Leviticus provides a large background to Mark 6:14–29, as does the book of Esther, neither provide all the details found in Mark's text.

CONCLUSION

Mark 6:14–29 has often confused its readers. It sticks out from the surrounding narrative and this has led some to conclude that this is not originally part of the text. However, it does serve a narrative purpose and pre-figures the fate of Jesus who is absent from this scene. Mark continues his strong reliance on Old Testament and apocryphal texts and skilfully interweaves his sources. First Corinthians 5 presents the only extant Christian writing that pre-dates Mark which deals with the same basic subject matter—the sexual immorality of a man living with a woman for whom he is forbidden to do so by Jewish law. This cannot be ignored.

Strong and weak connections were noted as was the presence of other sources for Mark. The similarities noted were consistent with the ancient literary methods of text absorption such as *varatio*, contemporization, and *contaminatio*. The level to which these texts appear to be related is consistent with conforming allusion and eclectic imitation. While there were differences between the texts these were largely explainable through Mark's narrative style and purpose and by the presence of other sources. These other sources do not make redundant the connections noted with 1 Cor 5:1–13 but rather provide the context in which these similarities need to be understood. Mark 6:14–29 emerges as a rich text with many literary sources among which is 1 Cor 5:1–13.

— 7 —

Comparison and Analysis of 1 Corinthians 11:2–34 and Mark 14:1–25

INTRODUCTION

THE EUCHARIST FEATURES HEAVILY in 1 Corinthians and Paul, in chapter 11, writes about how the Eucharist came about. It is strikingly similar to the inauguration of the Eucharist by Jesus in Mark 14. While the Eucharist in Luke may be closer to 1 Corinthians than Mark, it must still be recognized that 1 Corinthians and Mark share many similarities and it cannot merely be dismissed as being due to a common tradition as is often the case. Rather, the two texts must be analyzed in order to reveal the relationship between them, if any. Therefore, the texts surrounding the Eucharist have also been analyzed in order to provide any supporting evidence, if found, to a case for literary dependence.

The study of the Eucharist has generally focussed on the historical aspects of the passage and scholars have tried to find the original form of the Eucharist in Mark through redaction criticism. There is a division within scholarship in regard to how historical Mark's account is. Some view him as being largely historical while others have argued that the tradition was largely changed in light of Jesus' death and resurrection.[1] Attention has also been given to the meal in the ancient world and similarities that the

---

1. Hooker, *Gospel*, 339.

Eucharist has to other formal meal occasions.² Mark specifically mentions that the Eucharist took place on the night of the Passover and that it was a Passover meal. First Corinthians, while setting Jesus' death in a Passover context (1 Cor 5:7), does not place the Eucharist as such a time but does mention that it took place on the night that Jesus was betrayed and handed over. There are elements of Mark's text that are similar to the Passover and Jewish meals. Blessings, bread and hymns (v26) are all common in these circumstances.³

A major study on the Eucharist in the New Testament by Joachim Jeremias focussed on many aspects of the Eucharist accounts.⁴ Firstly, he tried to establish exactly what form of meal the Eucharist was. Although the synoptic gospels identify the Eucharist as a Passover meal, John does not. John locates the meal and the following events during Nisan 13 and 14 while the synoptic gospels place the event during Nisan 14 and 15. Therefore, in John, Jesus is crucified on the day of the preparation and the Last Supper/Eucharist cannot be a Passover meal.⁵ Jeremias suggests three ways that reconcile this. Firstly, it is possible that the synoptic gospels are right and John should be interpreted accordingly. Second, that John is right and the synoptic gospels should be interpreted accordingly. Third, that both John and the synoptic are right and should be interpreted accordingly.⁶

In determining whether or not the first Eucharist was a Passover meal, Jeremias explores various Jewish meal traditions such as Kiddus, Haburah and Essene meals. These are all rejected.⁷ In exploring the Passover context, Jeremias takes into consideration astronomy, the location of the meal, the room in which the meal was eaten, the time of the meal, those attending the meal, how those attending acted at the meal, the purity of the meal, the order of events, what was consumed, the type of wine, what was purchased for the meal, the donation to the poor, the singing of the hymn, what happened after the meal and the interpretation of the bread and wine.⁸ Jeremias concludes that the Last Supper/Eucharist was a Passover meal and that the connection to the Passover was lost in the early Church showing that the

---

2. Marcus, *Mark*, 2:965. See also, Leon-Dufour, *Sharing the Eucharistic Bread*.
3. Collins, *Mark*, 379. Marcus, *Mark*, 2:956. Noonan-Sabin, *Gospel*, 128.
4. Jeremias, *Eucharistic Words*.
5. Ibid., 16–20.
6. Ibid., 20–24. This latter view, that both were in some way correct, was one that was shared by many in the early twentieth century as Jeremias outlines.
7. Ibid., 26–36.
8. Ibid., 42–56.

description of the Last Supper did not originate with liturgical practice. He concludes that the accounts in the New Testament of the Eucharist are historical reminiscence.[9]

In favor of the Passover setting are many factors beyond the obvious mentions in the synoptic gospels. The night-time setting (1 Cor 11:23, Mark 14:17 and John 13:30) is consistent with a Passover meal, also eaten at night.[10] Jesus and his disciples are depicted as reclining which also happened at Passover meals as a symbol of liberty.[11] The breaking of bread, giving alms to the poor, drinking wine, singing hymns and a withdrawal to outside of Jerusalem are all consistent with a Passover setting.[12] Also, the explanation of the symbolism of the various parts of the meal is an important part of Passover remembrance.[13]

There are, however, many objections to classifying the Last Supper as a Passover meal. Firstly, the Passover was a family affair and Jesus shared the Last Supper with his disciples only; just men.[14] The word ἄρτος is incorrect for this setting with ζύμη being the more usual word for bread, or more specifically, unleavened bread used during the Passover.[15] There are no references to the paschal lamb or bitter herbs and no communal cups were used, rather there were individual ones.[16]

Scholars who maintain that this is sufficient evidence to suggest that the Last Supper/Eucharist was not a Passover meal offer alternative meal settings and argue that if the Eucharist was a Passover meal then it surely would have been celebrated annually in the early Church, which it was not.[17] Marshall points out that Jews gave thanks to God at every meal and, therefore, all meals were somewhat religious in nature. Special significance was given to meals connected with Passover and other festivals.[18] Therefore, if the Eucharist does not fit into a Passover model completely it still fits into the Jewish meal setting. The Last Supper/Eucharist would also fit

---

9. Ibid., 62.
10. O'Toole, "Last Supper," 236.
11. Ibid.
12. Ibid.
13. Marshall, "Lord's Supper," 570.
14. O'Toole, "Last Supper," 236.
15. Ibid.
16. Ibid.
17. Ibid.
18. Marshall, "Lord's Supper," 570.

into a Hellenistic meal setting. "Communal meals were important in both Judaism and Hellenistic religions. They served a social purpose in bringing the adherents together, and they function religiously in a variety of ways."[19]

Part of Jeremias' investigation is looking into which version of the Last Supper/Eucharist is the oldest. In discussing this, Jeremias notes that "The Markan tradition and the Pauline/Lukan tradition are independent of each other and do not go back to the same Greek source; the variations are too great for such a conclusion."[20]

This is based on Jeremias' assertion that Mark's account has certain Semitisms that Paul lacks and that, although written later than the account in 1 Corinthians, it actually represents the oldest form of the tradition.[21] This, of course, is problematic when Markan priority is accepted along with the unity of the text. This also shows a trend in scholarship that continues today in that Mark, followed by Matthew, represent one strand of tradition while 1 Corinthians and Luke represent another and that they are wholly unconnected.[22] In spite of this claim that these two traditions are unconnected, Jeremias admits that "On the other hand, we have seen that in their main features both forms are essentially the same. They go back therefore to a *common Eucharistic tradition lying behind both forms of the text . . .*"[23]

Therefore, according to Jeremias, while the traditions are independent, they do rely on an earlier common source. While Jeremias denies any common Greek source he allows for an Aramaic source behind both traditions. Jeremias' work, however, reflects a problem in dealing with these texts. Instead of attempting to reconcile the differences between the two texts it is all too tempting to say they are unconnected. However, the obvious similarities do not allow this to be done easily. Jeremias has attempted both options; he has tried to reconcile the differences while maintaining they are independent. This is simply contradictory.

As with many studies on the Last Supper/Eucharist conclusions can be influenced by a scholar's desire to view this important part of Christianity as historical and not part of a literary tradition. The religious stance of many scholars inevitably leads to an unconscious bias in favor of

---

19. Ibid.

20. Jeremias, *Eucharistic Words*, 186.

21. Ibid., 185–86.

22. Viewing two stands of Eucharistic tradition in the New Testament by 1 Corinthians/Luke and Mark/Matthew is somewhat commonplace within scholarship. Marshall, "The Lord's Supper," 570.

23. Jeremias, *Eucharistic Words*, 186.

historicity.²⁴ This is not to say that there is not necessarily an historical basis but rather that the literary aspects of such an account are not fully taken into account. Therefore, deciding how to view the Last Supper/Eucharist is a difficult task. A few scholars, however, have explored the literary aspects of the various traditions surrounding the Last Supper/Eucharist.

One possible literary background for the Last Supper/Eucharist accounts in the New Testament is the apocryphal text of *Joseph and Aseneth*. This possibility was explored by Christoph Burchard.²⁵ Although he does not see a literary connection between the New Testament Eucharist account and *Joseph and Aseneth* he sees it as providing a literary precedence for the scenes such as those with cultic meals and the imagery of bread and wine, both of which are also present in *Jos.An.* 8–21.²⁶ It is difficult to talk about dependence when dealing with *Joseph and Aseneth* as the large date range for its composition make it unclear in which direction influence would flow.

Turning to classical literature, Dennis R. MacDonald has found certain parallels and affinities between Homeric epics and the Gospel of Mark and the Last Supper/Eucharist is one of the areas on which MacDonald focuses. MacDonald sees a larger connection between the events surrounding the inauguration of the Eucharist and Odysseus' last meal before going to Hades in *Od.* 10.476–560.²⁷ Among the common elements which MacDonald points out are a shared meal with wine, both Odysseus' crew and Jesus' disciples sleep after the meal, both Odysseus and Jesus contemplate their respective futures, both despair and become resigned to their fate, both wake their companions, one of Odysseus' crew (Elpenor) dies while one of Jesus' disciples flees.²⁸ As striking as these similarities may seem, MacDonald has not been without critics.²⁹

However, it does reveal that the Last Supper/Eucharist does have literary parallels and that a literary source could be found in the absence of

---

24. O'Toole, "Last Supper," in *ABD* 4:234.
25. Burchard, "Importance," 102–34.
26. Ibid., 109–18.
27. MacDonald, *Homeric Epics,* 124–30.
28. Ibid., 130.

29. Winn provides a summary of the criticisms of MacDonald's work. See, Winn, *Elijah-Elisha,* 36–49. The main criticism listed are MacDonald's placement of Homer over that of the Jewish scriptures in terms of importance, the absence of obvious similarities, unpersuasive similarities, and subtle similarities being held in primacy over obvious ones from other texts.

further historical data. Accepting Markan priority to be correct, the account in Mark of the Eucharist is the second in composition behind the account in 1 Corinthians. Therefore, it is logical to investigate whether or not one relies on the other.

THE EUCHARIST AND ITS SURROUNDING TEXTS

Two larger sections will be analyzed comprising of 1 Cor 11:2–34 and Mark 14:1–25 which make up four small units within the texts, including the Eucharist. While 1 Cor 11:2–34 deals with the head dresses of women, their behavior at services and the abuses at the Lord's Supper, it is essentially one larger unit of text with four sub-units. First Corinthians 11:2 begins with Paul commending the Corinthians in their upholding of the traditions that were handed onto them by him. For Paul, an important issue here is the passing on of traditions and this is repeated in 11:23 and the same wording appears in both instances (παρέδωκα ὑμῖν). Therefore, while Paul may discuss both head dress and the Lord's Supper, he is also dealing with the passing on of tradition which brings this whole section of text together and creates one literary unit.

Turning to Mark 14:1–25, v. 1 is commonly held to be the beginning of the Passion narrative. The reason for stopping at v. 25 is that there is a decisive shift in location to the Mount of Olives and out of the setting of the meal. A change in location is a literary indicator that a new unit of text is beginning and the shift in v. 26 is indicative of this. While it is the case that Mark 14:1–25 does change locations throughout, the smaller subsections indicated by these location changes are tied together within the setting of the Passover which builds up to the Eucharist scene. Also, the Eucharist ends in v. 25 and the narrative moves into the next phase of the Passion, namely the arrest of Jesus.

Within their larger literary contexts 1 Cor 11:2–34 and Mark 14:1–25 play an important role. First Corinthians 11:2–34 is the part of a larger block of text that consists of 1 Cor 7–15 where Paul is concerned with answering the questions of the Corinthian church. Chapter eleven does, however, standout on its own and is wedged between two sub-blocks of text, namely 8:1–11:1 and 12:1–14:40.[30] Mark 14:1–25 forms the first part of a larger body of text, namely the Passion narrative which begins in v1. Therefore, although both texts are being treated somewhat in isolation here,

30. Conzelmann, *1 Corinthians*, 181–203. Fitzmyer, *First Corinthians*, 404–52.

Comparison and Analysis of 1 Corinthians 11:2–34 and Mark 14:1–25

they do form part of larger units within the closing stages of the respective documents as a whole.

First Corinthians 11 can be split into four rough sections which are as follows:

- 1 Cor 11:2–16—Women's behavior at services and head coverings.
- 1 Cor 11:17–22—Abuses at the Lord's Supper.
- 1 Cor 11:23–26—The Lord's Supper.
- 1 Cor 11:27–34—Unworthy partaking in the Lord's Supper.

Mark 14:1–25 can also be split into four sections which are as follows:

- Mark 14:1–11—The plot to kill Jesus and the anointing of Jesus in Simon's house.
- Mark 14:12–16—Preparations for the Passover.
- Mark 14:17–21—The Passover—Condemnation for the betrayer.
- Mark 14:22–25—The inauguration of the Eucharist.

The reason for not dividing 14:1–11 is that these eleven verses begin with the plot to kill Jesus and return to this subject at the end, tying the section together in the form of a chiastic structure. The scene at Simon's house is wedged between the two. It should also be noted that v1 begins by setting the scene two days before the Passover while v12 sets the scene on the first day of the Passover. It is now a different day and a different scene indicating that it is right to divide the text here and leaving 14:1–11 as one unit.[31]

First Corinthians 11:2–34	Mark 14:1–25[A]
Women and head coverings (11:2–16)	A woman anoints Jesus' head. "In memory of her" (14:1–11)
Division and abuses at the Lord's Supper, Coming together to eat (11:17–22)	Harmony in preparing for the Passover, Coming together to eat (14:12–16)
The Eucharist/Lord's Supper. 'In memory' (11:23–26)	The Eucharist/Lord's Supper (14:22–25)
Unworthy partaking at the Lord's Supper—Condemnation (11:27–34)	The betrayer is condemned (14:17–21)

A. The ordering of Mark has been altered to reflect the similarities found with 1 Corinthians.

---

31. Marcus illustrates that this section has a sandwich A'B'A structure. Marcus, *Mark*, 2:925.

The Quest for Mark's Sources

DETAILED ANALYSIS

WOMEN AND HEAD COVERINGS (1 COR 11:2–16 AND MARK 14:1–11)

In 1 Cor 1:2–16 Paul opens by commending the Corinthians for maintaining the traditions that he handed on to them. Paul then moves on to discuss head coverings for women during prayer. For men, it is a disgrace to cover their heads but for women it is a disgrace if their heads are left uncovered and he equates it to having their heads shaved. Paul says that for men it is a disgrace to cover their heads since they are a reflection of God while women are a reflection of men. Paul sees women as being subservient and not independent to men. Men and women come from each other and they both, ultimately, come from God. Paul then says that it is to a women's glory to wear her hair long as it was given to her as a covering. Finally Paul does not appeal to theology but to custom and says no church carries the custom of women praying with no head covering.

Mark's narrative begins two days before the Passover in 14:1–11 with the chief priests and scribes plotting against Jesus. Meanwhile, Jesus is in Bethany in the house of Simon the Leper. A woman comes to Jesus with a jar of expensive ointment with which she anoints him.[32] Others at the table see this as a waste, as it could be sold and the money given to the poor, and they scold her. Jesus says that what she has done is good as she has anointed his body before its burial. He then says that when the good news is proclaimed what she has done will be told in remembrance of her. This section then returns to where it began with the plot against Jesus and Judas Iscariot is revealed as the one who will betray him.

---

32. The text says it could be sold for about 300 denarii. One denarius was the average daily wage for a Palestinian agricultural worker during the first century C.E. and, therefore, this ointment nearly cost a year's worth of wages. The translation of μύρον here is debatable. In spite of the similarity to myrrh the words are unrelated. The Hebrew root of myrrh refers to the root of a plant while the root of μύρον means to anoint. A more accurate translation would be perfume. Perfumes of this time were oil based and fatty and therefore very thick and more consistent with what people today would class an ointment, although the application was as a perfume. Marcus also surmises that modern translators may be uncomfortable with the image of Jesus being heavily perfumed and, therefore, opt for the safer ointment translations. Marcus, *Mark*, 2:934–95.

Comparison and Analysis of 1 Corinthians 11:2-34 and Mark 14:1-25

Initial General Comparison

At the center of both texts is a controversy surrounding women. In 1 Corinthians it is to do with the head coverings of women during prayer while in Mark it is to do with the woman's anointing of Jesus' head with expensive ointment. In both cases the controversy surrounding woman has to do with the human head. The scene of the anointing in Mark has many elements that are not matched with 1 Corinthians and is sandwiched between another narrative thread about the plot to arrest and kill Jesus.

Literary Aspects of Mark 14:1-11

Parallels with Other Texts.

OLD TESTAMENT

"Mark's account of Jesus' suffering, death and resurrection in chapters 14-16 is suffused with Old Testament citations and allusions to an extent unparalleled in the rest of the narrative, a frequency that reflects the primitive Christian conviction that Christ died and was raised on the third day in accordance with the scriptures."[33] The web of citations, allusions and parallels to the Old Testament in Mark 14:1-11 is large and what is presented are only the most obvious of these. There may yet be many unidentified allusions and parallels. Straight away in 14:1 there is a parallel to Hos 6:2 which beings: ὑγιάσει ἡμᾶς μετὰ δύο ἡμέρας. Mark 14:1 begins in a similar fashion: Ἦν δὲ τὸ πάσχα καὶ τὰ ἄζυμα μετὰ δύο ἡμέρας. Both contain the identical phrase μετὰ δύο ἡμέρας. What makes this parallel more intriguing is that immediately after in Hos 6:2 the text speaks of being raised on the third day. The passion in Mark ends with the finding of the empty tomb on the third day and here, at the very beginning of the passion narrative it has already been foreshadowed through this allusion.[34]

Also in 14:1 is an allusion to Ps 10:7-8 (LXX 9:28-29) which mentions cursing, deceit and an ambush in terms of the righteous sufferer which will be incorporated into Mark many times throughout the passion narrative. The vocabulary used here is similar to that of Mark 14:1. Both use

---

33. Marcus, *Way of the Lord*, 153.
34. Marcus, *Mark*, 2.932.

The Quest for Mark's Sources

δόλος (treachery) and ἀποκτείνω (to kill) and Jesus is cast in the role of the righteous sufferer.[35]

Turning to the anointing itself, it evokes many Old Testament anointing scenes such as 1 Sam 10:1 and 2 Kgs 9:3, 6. First Samuel 10:1 depicts the anointing of Saul, while 2 Kgs 9:3, 6 depicts the instructions to and the anointing of Jehu as king of Israel. In these texts a flask of oil is taken and poured on the anointed one's head. It is an act highly associated with the anointing of the kings of Israel. Jesus is not only the righteous sufferer but is also the anointed king of Israel. The act of remembrance of the good deed of anointing is something which finds a parallel in Neh 13:14, 22 where good deeds are also remembered.

Apocrypha

Turning to apocryphal texts some more parallels can be found. Firstly, 1 Esd 1:17 (LXX) which reads καὶ ἠγάγοσαν οἱ υἱοὶ Ἰσραὴλ οἱ εὑρεθέντες ἐν τῷ καιρῷ τούτῳ τὸ πάσχα καὶ τὴν ἑορτὴν τῶν ἀζύμων ἡμέρας ἑπτά. This is very similar to Mark 14:1: Ἦν δὲ τὸ πάσχα καὶ τὰ ἄζυμα μετὰ δύο ἡμέρας. καὶ ἐζήτουν οἱ ἀρχιερεῖς καὶ οἱ γραμματεῖς πῶς αὐτὸν ἐν δόλῳ κρατήσαντες ἀποκτείνωσιν.

The notion of remembrance in Mark 14:9 finds a parallel in 4 Macc 17:8 which speaks of inscriptions on grave markers as a remembrance (εἰς μνείαν). Acts of remembrance were associated with graves and funerals. Considering the events leading to Jesus' death are in motion, this parallel takes on an important significance.

Classical Texts

Parallels to classical literature are somewhat harder to find than the obvious Old Testament allusions yet some work has been done in this area. Dennis MacDonald has identified a series of parallels between Mark 13:1—14:11 and the *Od.* 19. This series of parallels culminates in the anointing of the central character. In *Od.* 19, Odysseus has his feet washed by Eurycleia who also anoints his head with oil. She recognizes him as her king. Odysseus

---

35. Marcus, *Way of the Lord*, 172.

and Eurycleia then discuss the betrayal of the servant while in Mark, one of Jesus' own disciples is preparing to betray him.[36] These parallels are striking.

Detailed Comparison

Context

The contexts of both texts are similar as both come at the beginning of a larger unit of text. First Corinthians 11:2–16 is part of Paul's discussion of the abuses of the Lord's Supper which will build up to a description of the event itself. Similarly, Mark 14:1–11 is also the start of a new unit of text, namely the Passion narrative.

Theme

In both sections women play a key role and are the central theme of 1 Cor 11:2–16. While Mark's text is not primarily concerned with women it is one of the section's themes along with wealth, poverty and the plot to kill Jesus. People are offended not by the presence of a woman in Mark but by her seemingly reckless use of a very expensive ointment which could be sold and the money given to the poor. However, it is the image of the woman that the reader is left with at the end of the episode as the reader is meant to remember her and not the ointment.[37] In both 1 Corinthians and Mark women are connected very much to the human head. In 1 Cor 11:2–16 Paul is concerned with women and head coverings. Whatever the meaning of Paul's text, it is unusual in combining an emphasis on women and Christ's role as head.[38] Paul states that it dishonors women to not have their head covered during prayer. In Mark 14:1–11, while not dealing with head coverings, a woman anoints the head of Jesus. Both women and the human head are part of a common theme and this is a rare occurrence. It should also be noted that Paul speaks of Christ being the head of every

---

36. MacDonald, *Homeric Epics*, 111–19.

37. The phrase 'in memory of her' has sparked significant debate including the work of feminist theologian Elisabeth Fiorenza. See, Fiorenza, *In Memory of Her*.

38. Fitzmyer sums up the various scholarly viewpoints concerning the meaning of this section. Fitzmyer, *First Corinthians*, 405–7. Eph 5:21–24 contains a similar collection of themes.

man. In Mark, it is Jesus' head that is being anointed. Christ/Jesus' head is, therefore, at the center of both, although with different emphases.

There is also a thematic similarity towards the end of these two sections. First Corinthians 11:16 mentions αἱ ἐκκλησίαι τοῦ θεοῦ (the churches of God) which presumably means the entire Christian world while Mark 14:9 mentions ὅλον τὸν κόσμον (the whole world). Both sections contain an appeal to the larger world/church and women, in both cases, play an important role in this larger appeal, although the nature of their role is different in each text.

Also, in both there are people who object to something and are acting contentiously. In 1 Cor 11:16 Paul says that if people are going to be contentious over the issue of women and head coverings then they should know that it is not the custom for them to be uncovered. Paul clearly anticipates people continuing to argue over this issue. In Mark 14:4 those present at the meal are angry and the expensive oil is being wasted in their view. Essentially, they are being contentious. In both, this contention is wrong and corrected by Paul in 1 Corinthians and by Jesus in Mark.

The story recounted in Mark 14:3–9 may also provide an answer to a question concerning the relationship between the two Eucharistic texts. Mark's version of the Eucharist omits the Corinthian call to remembrance (τοῦτο ποιεῖτε εἰς τὴν ἐμὴν ἀνάμνησιν—1 Cor 11:24). Remembrance, however, is found in Mark 14:9. Jesus says that the woman's actions will be told in memory of her (εἰς μνημόσυνον αὐτῆς). The word Mark uses for remembrance/memory is the noun μνημόσυνον which is very rare and only found three times in the New Testament. Paul uses the noun ἀνάμνησις which carries the same meaning as μνημόσυνον. It may seem odd that Mark would elect to use a different word, if he is dependent on 1 Corinthians here, but this is perfectly acceptable and expected in ancient writing, particularly in Greco-Roman writing techniques where writers were discouraged from whole-sale absorption of one text into another—this was considered plagiarism when not cited.[39] Thus, the moving of it from one place to another is consistent with ancient literary methods. Also, remembrance is not the theological concern of Mark in regard to the Eucharist. Rather, Mark wishes to emphasize and look forward to Jesus' coming death and resurrection. However, why would Mark not simply omit reference to remembrance altogether? The answer may be simply that he chose to place it before the Eucharist itself in order to dramatically build to the Eucharist scene. The

---

39. See Cicero, *Opt. gen* 14, *Fin.* 3.4.15; Quintilian, *Inst.* 1.9.2; Horace, *Ars.* 133.

breaking of the vase and pouring of the ointment over Jesus is reminiscent of the breaking of bread and pouring out of wine.[40] Thus, Mark is prefiguring events to come which will also be remembered as will be the woman.

Action/Plot and Order

In terms of action/plot, there are some affinities in that both have action unfold around the themes already noted. In both, the house is an important setting. Jesus is eating in the house of Simon the Leper while Paul is discussing early Christian gatherings which were held in houses, although not explicitly stated here. Women are central in both, as is Christ's head, although they are dealt with in very different ways. Both scenes also end with an appeal to a larger context. Paul appeals to traditions and universal customs while Mark says the woman will be remembered wherever the good news is proclaimed—essentially, universally. However, genre differences preclude plot similarities in many instances.

In terms of order, there is little to discuss as the themes that are shared by both do not follow a similar order.

Vocabulary

Many of the shared words found are connected to the common themes. Both γυνή and κεφαλή appear multiple times in 1 Cor 11:2–16 and both appear in Mark 14:3. The verbs ἔχω and θέλω appear in both texts as does the verb δίδωμι and its compound form παραδίδωμι.

Both 1 Corinthians and Mark tell of contentious/angry people and both use unusual vocabulary to express this. Paul uses φιλόνεικος and this is its only occurrence in the New Testament and it only appears once in the LXX (Ezek 3:7) and Mark uses ἀγανακτέω which only appears seven times in the New Testament and four times in apocryphal texts. First Corinthians 11:26 in part reads δέ τις δοκεῖ φιλόνεικος εἶναι. Mark 14:4, in a similar fashion, reads ἦσαν δέ τινες ἀγανακτοῦντες. Similar phrasing is used in both, clustered around the image of contentious/angry people.

---

40. Noonan-Sabin, *Reopening the Word*, 193.

The Quest for Mark's Sources

Completeness

Given the ambiguity of 1 Cor 11:2–16 it is impossible to claim that all its major elements are reflected in Mark. However, many elements were common to both which has been observed.

Assessment and Conclusion

In assessing the data collected, many similarities between these two sections were noted which can be summarized as follows:

- Both have an assembly/house setting.
- Both have women at the center of the text.
- In both, heads are covered (with oil in Jesus' case).
- The head of Christ is important in both.
- Both end with an appeal to a larger world.
- Both refer to unnamed people who are contentious.
- Both share the vocabulary γυνή, κεφαλή, ἔχω, θέλω, δίδωμι, and its compound form παραδίδωμι.

Not every aspect of Mark 14:1–11 is matched by 1 Cor 11:2–16. For example, there are no parallels with the material that forms the chiasm in this section of Mark. This material is sourced elsewhere and three distinct elements of Mark's text can be seen. Firstly, there is the basic Markan narrative of Jesus' life and ministry and here Mark enters the most important and climactic part of this story, in the form of the Passion. Secondly, there is a complex web of Old Testament allusions and parallels to Homeric epics. The Old Testament material provides Mark with much of his narrative and in particular the chiastic material that finds no parallels with 1 Cor 11:2–16. Lastly there are the affinities and similarities noted with 1 Corinthians.

ABUSES AT THE LORD'S SUPPER: COMING TOGETHER TO EAT (1 COR 11:17–22 AND MARK 14:12–16)

In contrast to the opening of 1 Cor 11:2–16, Paul begins 1 Cor 11:17–22 not with commending but saying that he does not commend them. This is in relation to coming together to eat and following his instructions. Paul repeats the report that there are divisions amongst the Corinthian church but while granting the need for difference of viewpoints, he goes on to say that when they come together to eat it is not really for the Lord's Supper but rather some go before others and some have nothing to eat while others get drunk. Paul asks a series of questions about their conduct and ends as he started by repeating that he does not commend them.

Mark 14:12–16 begins in a similar fashion to 14:1–11 in that the scene is set out in a time relative to the Passover. Now it is the first day of unleavened bread and the disciples ask Jesus about the preparations for the Passover. Jesus then sends the disciples to meet and follow a man carrying a jar of water. Wherever this man enters the disciples are to ask the owner of the house where the guest room is so that Jesus may eat the Passover with his disciples. Jesus says that this man will show them a large upstairs room already furnished. The disciples then set out to do as Jesus said and make the preparations for the Passover.

Initial General Comparison

Immediately apparent is that both sections are set within the context of a shared meal. For Paul it is the Lord's Supper and for Mark it is the Passover. Both, however, show opposite approaches to the meal. In Paul, people are not coming together in the proper spirit of the meal and there is division in Corinth as some are going without food while others are getting drunk. Mark, on the other hand, presents a contrasting scene of a united preparation for the Passover. What unfolds is exactly as Jesus has said. For Paul, this is not the case—the Corinthians have not been following his instructions. In essence, 1 Corinthians shows how not to respond to instructions concerning a meal while in Mark it is shown how to respond correctly. The sections, in general, appear complementary to each other.

Literary Aspects of Mark 14:12–16

Parallels with other texts.

Old Testament

It was noted when dealing with Mark 14:1–11 that the anointing of Jesus was reminiscent of Old Testament anointing scenes such as the anointing of Saul in 1 Sam 10:1 and the anointing of Jehu by Elisha's disciple in 2 Kgs

9:6. Here the allusion to Saul continues with an allusion to 1 Sam 10:1–10 where Samuel tells Saul that he will meet a series of people.[41]

Another connection comes from the many Old Testament scenes of women carrying water such as Gen 24:11–21; Exod 2:16; and 1 Sam 9:11. However, it is possibly a man in Mark who is carrying the water, something which in the Old Testament is almost exclusively reserved for women.[42] There are, however, some instances where men are found carrying water such as Deut 29:10–11 and Josh 9:21–27. Greco-Roman artists depicted male slaves carrying jugs of water, although whether or not the man in Mark 14:12–16 should be understood in this context is unclear.[43]

Classical Texts

As with Mark 14:1–11, MacDonald sees the influence of the *Odyssey* here.[44] In the *Od.* 10.100–103 and 105–16 Odysseus sends some of his companions to go and learn who the men on the Laestrygonian shore are when they land there. The companions meet a girl drawing water from a well, and they follow her to a high-roofed house where they are seized and prepared to be eaten. Both the *Odyssey* and Mark lead to what MacDonald terms a "cannibalistic feast."[45]

Detailed Comparison

Context

The context of both is similar. Within the four units in both texts connected to the Eucharist, both occur in the second place, and in both instances the openings mirror that of their predecessor. In 1 Cor 11:17–22 Paul is discussing the abuses of the Lord's Supper, a remembrance meal of the Last Supper, while in Mark 14:12–16 the disciples are preparing for the Passover, an important Jewish meal, which will be Jesus' last before his death.

---

41. Collins, *Mark*, 647.
42. Marcus, *Mark*, 2:945. The word ἄνθρωπος is somewhat ambiguous and may not mean man but rather person.
43. Ibid.
44. MacDonald, *Homeric Epics*, 120–23.
45. Ibid., 123.

Comparison and Analysis of 1 Corinthians 11:2–34 and Mark 14:1–25

Theme

Here, Paul is instructing the Corinthians just as Jesus is instructing the disciples in Mark. Their instruction is different but both texts revolve around people coming together to eat in some form of table fellowship. The picture Paul paints of Corinth is one of disunity and chaos with people coming together and abusing the institution of the Lord's Supper. They are coming together but not in the proper spirit of the occasion. This, as Paul will point out, is a time for remembrance. In Mark 14:12–16 there are also people preparing to come together in table fellowship. The scene here is quite different to the scene in Corinth and is calm and peaceful. There is none of the sense of confusion that is found in Corinth, nobody is going without and nobody is drinking to excess. Both are building to their account of Jesus' last meal with his disciples before his arrest, trial and execution.

Action/Plot and Order

In terms of action/plot, both are building to the description of the Last Supper and they do this in a similar way. Paul begins (11:17–19) in a general way, condemning their actions and their fall into division. Then in the second part of the text (11:20–22), he repeats the word coming together (συνερχομένων) and moves in closer to the problem and describes what is actually happening—he begins outside the problem and then moves inside of it. Similarly in Mark, the disciples ask about the preparations and Jesus begins to instruct them. Again there are two uses of compound forms of ἔρχομαι here (ἀπέρχομαι in 14:12 and εἰσέρχομαι in 14:14). This action moves from the outside to the inside, outside the house to inside it. Both share the movement, but Mark gives a clearer sense of a movement that is progressive, a narrative that moves from going away to going in.

The contrast between the divisions and harmony in these sections finds precedent in the contrast, discussed in chapter 5 concerning the divisions in Corinth and the unity in Mark. In 1 Cor 1:10 the divisions amongst the community were signified with the word σχίσμα and the same is the case here in 1 Cor 11:18. Similarly in Mark the unified following of Jesus is expressed in the verb ἀκολουθέω and this happens here in Mark 14:13 also. Thus the contrast between σχίσμα and ἀκολουθέω occurs in both 1 Corinthians and Mark twice, once at the start of each text (1 Cor 1:10; Mark 1:18) and once here in the build up to the Eucharist (1 Cor 11:18; Mark 14:13).

In terms of order Mark loosely follows the order of 1 Cor 11 but the genre differences make shared order an unlikely possibility and all the more significant when it occurs.

Vocabulary

In terms of vocabulary, these two sections share little beyond πρῶτος, ἐσθίω, and, λέγω. The verb to eat would be expected as both sections are set within the context of the meal.

Completeness

To what extent is every major aspect of 1 Cor 11:17–22 matched by Mark 14:12–16? Many elements find a match, both share the context of the meal, both are leading up to a description of the Last Supper/Eucharist and both share a common transition of moving from outside to the inside. The disunity described by Paul is matched by Mark as a contrasting harmony. Paul is describing events at meals while in Mark it is the preparation for a meal that is narrated. The lack of attentiveness to one another at the Corinthian meal is matched, again in a contrasting way, by the unobtrusive service provided by the person carrying the water and the householder who prepared the room.

Assessment and Conclusion

The similarities noted can be summarized as follows:
- Both are set in the context of a meal.
- Both are building to a description of the Lord's Supper.
- Both move from outside to the inside.
- Both share the vocabulary πρῶτος, ἐσθίω, and λέγω.
- Mark's picture of harmonious following (ἀκολουθέω) not only gives a precise contrast to the Corinthians' division (σχίσμα), it also continues the connection of these two words found in 1 Cor 1:10 and Mark 1:18.
- The unobtrusive service of the two people encountered in Mark gives a contrast to the loutish behavior in Corinth.

Comparison and Analysis of 1 Corinthians 11:2-34 and Mark 14:1-25

Some of these parallels, such as vocabulary, are general in nature but they follow on from the parallels noted in the previous section and will continue into the next, forming a chain of similarities. Underneath this chain is a web of Old Testament allusions, parallels with the *Odyssey* and Mark's underlying narrative of the life and ministry of Jesus. It is in this context that any similarities need to be viewed. First Corinthians is clearly not a main source here, yet certain strands and affinities can be seen woven into the fabric of the narrative.

THE EUCHARIST ACCOUNTS (1 COR 11:23-26 AND MARK 14:22-25)

As these are the climactic sections of both units of text under investigation it will be necessary to analyze both texts in more detail.

First Corinthians 11:23-26 is an important part of 1 Cor 11 and is the climax of Paul's discussion of the Lord's Supper. He recounts the Lord's Supper as he knows it in an effort to bring the Corinthians back to the proper observance of the event. The overall tone of the passage is one of remembrance or more specifically correct remembrance.[46] For Paul, tradition is key and he says that he passed this tradition onto the Corinthians as it was passed onto him by the Lord. Paul clearly views this as authoritative and sees this as adding weight to his argument.[47] This "passing on" motif goes back to the beginning of chapter 11 when Paul refers to keeping the traditions he has passed on (1 Cor 11:2).[48]

Paul introduces this section while discussing the proper observance of the Lord's Supper and states what he handed onto the Corinthians. Verse 23 serves to introduce the description of the Lord's Supper as Paul knows it. After announcing that he received this tradition from the Lord he places the event on the night that Jesus was betrayed but he does not name the betrayer. He mentions that Jesus first took the loaf, gave thanks and then broke it. Next there is one of the few occasions that Paul mentions any words of Jesus, some of the earliest in Christian literature. Jesus says Τοῦτό μού ἐστιν τὸ σῶμα τὸ ὑπὲρ ⌜ὑμῶν· τοῦτο ποιεῖτε εἰς τὴν ἐμὴν ἀνάμνησιν (1 Cor 11:24). What should be noted here is that Jesus states that his body is "for you." Then there is the important call to repeat this event in remembrance.

---

46. Collins, *Mark*, 654.
47. Ciampa and Rosner, *First Corinthians*, 548.
48. Ibid., 549.

Paul is concerned with the proper remembrance of this event and a call to remembrance is found in Paul's version of the Lord's Supper. Next, Jesus takes the cup (its contents are not stated) and says Τοῦτο τὸ ποτήριον ἡ καινὴ διαθήκη ἐστὶν ἐν τῷ ἐμῷ αἵματι· τοῦτο ποιεῖτε, ὁσάκις ἐὰν πίνητε, εἰς τὴν ἐμὴν ἀνάμνησιν (1 Cor 11:25). Just as the bread was linked to his body so the cup is linked to blood and also to a new covenant. Following this is a further call to repeat these actions in remembrance. In v. 26 Paul interprets these actions and words. By eating the bread and drinking from the cup Christians are proclaiming Jesus' death until he returns. From this it can be seen that Paul's interpretation of the Lord's Supper is linked with the death of Jesus and his eschatological return.

Likewise, for Mark, the inauguration of the Eucharist is one of the most important parts of the narrative along with the crucifixion. It is the last time Jesus is together with his disciples and it is the last peaceful moment before his arrest and crucifixion. Mark's focus is on foreshadowing Jesus' death. Mark is seeking to "... interpret Jesus' death beforehand in the context of the Gospel as a whole."[49]

This section of Mark is climactic and is basically the calm before the storm in the narrative. Mark sets up the inauguration of the Eucharist as a Passover meal and the importance of the Passover runs throughout chapter 14. The beginning of Mark 14 places the timing of events in relation to the coming Passover and vv. 12–21 (the preparation for the Passover and the condemnation of the betrayer) acts as an extended introduction to the event that would become central to Christian worship in the early church. Mark locates the Eucharist on the night that Jesus was arrested. The text of the inauguration of the Eucharist begins in earnest in v. 22 when Jesus takes the bread, blesses it and breaks it. He then gives it to them and says, Λάβετε, τοῦτό ἐστιν τὸ σῶμά μου. Here Jesus explicitly links the bread to his body. Following this he takes the cup, gives thanks, gives it to the disciples and they all drink from it (it is unclear whether Jesus drinks from it). He then says, Τοῦτό ἐστιν τὸ αἷμά μου τῆς διαθήκης τὸ ἐκχυννόμενον ὑπὲρ πολλῶν. ἀμὴν λέγω ὑμῖν ὅτι οὐκέτι οὐ μὴ πίω ἐκ τοῦ γενήματος τῆς ἀμπέλου ἕως τῆς ἡμέρας ἐκείνης ὅταν αὐτὸ πίνω καινὸν ἐν τῇ βασιλείᾳ τοῦ θεοῦ (14:24–25). He links his blood to the covenant which is "poured out for many." Jesus then foreshadows his own death by stating that he will not drink wine again until he is in the "kingdom of God."

---

49. Collins, *Mark*, 654.

Comparison and Analysis of 1 Corinthians 11:2–34 and Mark 14:1–25

Initial General Comparison

When comparing the two texts there are many close similarities. They both have many of the same plot points in the progression of the Eucharist. In both, Jesus takes a loaf of bread and either gives thanks or blesses the bread. Both link bread and body and both link blood and cup after Jesus takes the cup. The cup is also linked with covenant in both. There are also some differences which cannot be ignored in such a small amount of text. In 1 Corinthians, Jesus does not give the bread or wine to the disciples and while he says the bread is "for you" the wine does not come with a similar clause. In Mark the opposite is found as the wine is "poured out for many" and bread is not given the same status. There is a contrast here and the wine is given greater importance in Mark's text. The most significant difference between the two texts is that Mark lacks the call to repeat the event in remembrance which, as has been seen, finds a parallel in the anointing scene. However, it is in these two texts that the most prominent similarities so far have been seen.

Literary Aspects of Mark 14:22–25

Parallels with Other Texts

OLD TESTAMENT

Mark locates the inauguration of the Eucharist at the Passover and the first Passover in Exod 12:1–29 immediately comes to mind as does the establishment of the covenant with Moses and especially the blood of the covenant in Exod 24:1–8.

Zechariah has also influenced Mark here. He mentioned the blood of the covenant (αἵματι διαθήκης—Zech 9:11) and Zech 14:9, like Mark 14:25, looks forward to a future day with God as King.[50]

Isaiah plays an important role here also and the idea of blood being poured out, for many, finds an origin in Isa 53:12 which speaks of the suffering servant pouring himself out to death for others. The suffering servant is also handed over as Jesus is (Mark 14:21 and Isa 53:6, 12).[51] This "... web of

---

50. Marcus, *Way of the Lord*, 157.
51. Ibid.

OT allusions"[52] began in Mark 1:1 and is still continuing at this late stage in the gospel and will continue until the end, underpinning much of the text.

CLASSICAL TEXTS

Here too, MacDonald sees an influence from the *Odyssey*. This influence starts in Mark 14:17 at the beginning of the Passover and extends to v. 52 after the betrayal and arrest of Jesus and comes from the *Od.* 10.476–560.[53] Before Odysseus' journeys to Hades, he feasts one last time with his crew and they participate in a large meal which includes wine in a fashion similar to Jesus and his disciples.[54] However, this similarity is very general in nature, yet the larger chain offers some very intriguing parallels.

Detailed Comparison

Context

The context for both accounts of the Eucharist is that they come at the end of a certain amount of build up. In 1 Corinthians, the opening of the account mirrors 11:2 in that they both refer to tradition. The previous section also mirrored 11:2 in reference to praise. The account comes after Paul first praises the Corinthians for the maintaining of the traditions and after he does not praise their following of instructions. He commends, condemns and then gives them the tradition so there can be no doubt as to what the tradition is, which Paul sees as handed down to him. The account of the Eucharist will lead into his discussion of participating in the remembrance meal, the Lord's Supper, in an unworthy manner.

Similarly in Mark, the account of the Eucharist comes at the end of a certain amount of build up, beginning with the start of the Passion narrative in 14:1 (although the Eucharist has been foreshadowed throughout the gospel many times). The plot to kill Jesus is in motion and he has been anointed king. The disciples have gone and prepared for the Passover in an enigmatic fashion and the scene has been set for this climactic piece. Jesus has also foretold that one of his disciples will betray him, causing more tension in the narrative, although it has already been revealed to be Judas.

---

52. Marcus, *Mark*, 2:966.
53. MacDonald, *Homeric Epics*, 130.
54. Ibid.

Comparison and Analysis of 1 Corinthians 11:2–34 and Mark 14:1–25

Theme

Turning to theme, both texts present unity around the sharing of bread. In 1 Corinthians one community shares in this remembrance and in Mark one group of disciples shares in it. The cup reaffirms this unity as it is a cup of the new covenant, a covenant that binds people together under Christ.[55] That people are not acting appropriately in Corinth disrupts this unity and Paul seeks to restore it.[56] The unity is disrupted in the Markan account also as, while the bread and wine are unifying symbols, Jesus has just revealed that one of his disciples will betray him—thus creating disunity.

There are, however, certain differences in them that should be noted. The account in 1 Corinthians is reminiscence while in Mark it is part of a progressing narrative. Paul, therefore, places much more emphasis on remembrance than Mark. Also, Paul is recounting the Last Supper so as to remind the Corinthians of the proper way to come together—the Lord's Supper, as opposed to the Last Supper is, in itself, an act of remembrance. This motif permeates the whole account in 1 Corinthians and the surrounding context. Paul may be thinking of the Passover which was also a day of remembrance (Exod 12:14)[57] while the links to the Passover are obvious in Mark the aspect of remembrance is not as strong and the call to remembrance is absent, although remembrance is present, close by, in the anointing scene earlier in Mark 14.

Action/Plot and Order

In terms of action/plot and order these two accounts share much. In both, Jesus takes the bread, blesses it and gives/breaks it. He also takes the cup which is connected to a new covenant in both. Both have an eschatological element in that both look to a time beyond the present one. The order of the Eucharist is almost identical in both.

---

55. Ciampa and Rosner, *First Corinthians*, 552.

56. Ibid.

57. Leitzmann sees this remembrance as being part of the tradition of Greek memorial feasts for the dead. See Lietzmann, *Mass*, 238. Jeremias rejects this. Jeremias, *Eucharistic Words*, 238.

The Quest for Mark's Sources

Vocabulary

Both accounts of the Eucharist share much vocabulary and this can be of no surprise as both are narrating the same event. The first similarity that is found is Jesus taking the loaf of bread. Paul includes this in his introduction of the Lord's Supper and ἔλαβεν ἄρτον forms a transition between the location of the event in time and the actual order of events themselves. It is firmly in the past tense and Paul uses the aorist to express this. Mark also puts the taking of the loaf in this tense but in its participle form, thus emphasizing the flow of events and progressing the narrative. Paul is not writing a narrative in quite the same way and needs a transitional passage (v. 23) to temporarily transform his theological letter into narrative. This would be redundant in Mark and there is, therefore, no corresponding passage. The noun εὐχαριστήσας appears in both texts in the same form but in different places in the narrative. In 1 Corinthians it appears in v24 and is associated with the bread—Jesus gives thanks and then breaks the bread. In Mark it appears in v. 23 and is associated with the cup. In Paul's version there is no thanks associated with the cup although it is implied. First Corinthians 14:25 begins ὡσαύτως καὶ meaning "in the same way" implying that he also gave thanks here. Mark elects to use εὐλογέω here instead of εὐχαριστέω. While εὐλογέω can be used to mean giving thanks, it is generally a blessing. Mark may be giving the bread an extra layer of significance here that 1 Corinthians lacks.

The use of the verb εἰμί in linking bread with body and cup with blood may also indicate a connection between the two accounts in that its use reveals how the bread and wine being likened to body and blood should be interpreted. In both accounts Jesus states that the bread *is* his body. This is conveyed through the use of εἰμί in both. The use of εἰμί makes it clear that this is not in a literal sense but rather as a simile when used in an explanation.[58]

Steps of the Eucharist in 1 Cor 11:23–26	Steps of the Eucharist in Mark 14:22–25
Paul introduces the Eucharist account (v. 23)	
Jesus takes the bread (v. 23)	Jesus takes the bread (v. 22)
He gives thanks and breaks it (v. 24)	He blesses it and gives it to the disciples (v. 22)

---

58. Ciampa and Rosner, *First Corinthians*, 550.

Comparison and Analysis of 1 Corinthians 11:2–34 and Mark 14:1–25

He says that the bread is his body (v. 24)	He says that the bread is his body (v. 22)
"Do this in remembrance of me" (v. 24)	
Jesus takes the cup (v. 25)	Jesus takes the cup (v. 23)
	He thanks and gives it to the disciples (v. 23)
The cup is a new covenant in his blood (v. 25)	Wine is the blood of the covenant (v. 24)
"Do this in remembrance of me" (v. 25)	
Paul looks forward to the eschatological future (v. 26)	Jesus looks forward to the eschatological future (v. 25)

Completeness

Virtually every element of 1 Cor 11:23–26 finds an almost exact match in Mark 14:22–25. While Mark lacks an introductory passage and a call to remembrance every other element is matched with only very minor differences.

Assessment and Conclusion

In assessing the data collected, the most striking parallels seen in the investigation have been noted and can be summarized as follows:
- Both are located on the night Jesus is betrayed.
- Both share the same plot—Jesus' final meal.
- The order of events in both is almost identical.
- Both share much of the same vocabulary.

Almost every element of Paul's account finds a match in the Markan account and the differences are intelligible. The amount of shared vocabulary, in normal circumstances, would almost certainly warrant a conclusion of literary dependence. Yet, modern scholarship has preferred to attribute this to a shared oral/liturgical tradition. In principle some such tradition is possible but there is no access to it and in the present case the involving of such a tradition is not necessary. Mark's account of the Eucharist may be explained more readily on a literary basis; namely that Mark used 1 Corinthians as one component of the composition of this scene. Paul's text and Mark's are the two oldest accounts available of the Eucharist tradition and they share many elements. Strands of many diverse texts find their way into Mark. In this instance 1 Cor 11:23–26 presents the closest possible source to Mark. No other text can account for the material in Mark 14:22–25 in a more satisfactory manner.

UNWORTHY EATING: SELF EXAMINATION AND JUDGEMENT (1 COR 11:27–34 AND MARK 14:17–21)

Following the account of the Last Supper Paul returns to his previous discussion about what happens when the Corinthians come together to celebrate the Lord's Supper and the consequences of not participating in the proper manner. Paul asks the Corinthians to examine themselves before they participate in the Lord's Supper as those who do not, bring judgement down upon themselves. It is because some have not done this that they became ill and died. By not judging themselves and being judged by the Lord they are being disciplined in order that they not be condemned along with the world. Paul finishes by giving further instructions that if someone is hungry they should eat at home so that when they come together it will not bring about their condemnation.

Mark 14:1 began two days before the Passover and Mark 14:12 started on the first day of the Passover and this section begins in the evening of that day. While the disciples are seated at the start of the meal Jesus announces that one of them will betray him. The disciples become distressed and begin to question themselves as to whom Jesus is referring. Jesus confirms that it is one of the twelve who will betray him and says that it would be better for that person to have never been born rather than betray the Son of Man.

Initial General Comparison

Again both texts are set within the context of a meal. Paul concludes his discussion of the abuses of the Lord's Supper while in Mark the Passover meal has begun. Connected to this in both is unworthy participation. The abuses in Corinth show that some are participating in the meal in an unworthy manner while in Mark, someone who is eating the meal with Jesus will ultimately betray him and is, therefore, an unworthy participant. Both also contain self-examination. In 1 Corinthians Paul asks the Corinthians to examine themselves before participating in the meal while in Mark, Jesus' revelation that a betrayer sits at the table provokes self-examination on the part of the disciples. A judgment in both is connected to this self-examination. Paul says that judgement by the Lord is necessary and one cannot judge oneself. In Mark, Jesus judges the betrayer saying that it would be better for that person to have never been born.

Literary Aspects of Mark 14:17–21

Parallels with Other Texts

OLD TESTAMENT

The verb παραδίδωμι (to hand over) is common in the LXX and is used to describe God's handing over and delivering people to their deaths (Deut 2:33, Josh 10:8, Judg 8:3, 1 Sam 17:47). The implication for Mark is that this is a divinely ordained act.

Isaiah's account of the suffering servant is alluded to again here. In Isa 53:10 God gives up the suffering servant to death. In Mark, Jesus makes it clear that he is being given up to death and Mark wants this to evoke the image of the suffering servant as whom Jesus is being presented.

A recurring theme is the righteous sufferer of the Psalms. In Ps 41:9 (LXX 40:10) the suffering servant speaks of his "bosom friend." This friend shares the sufferer's bread and then lifts his heel against him. This allusion in Mark's scene is striking. Judas has been cast in the role of this "bosom friend" who shares Jesus' bread and then betrays him. This is a continuation of Jesus' connection to the righteous sufferer found earlier when dealing with Mark 14:1–11

Detailed Comparison

Context

Both sections come very close to a description of the Last Supper. In the case of 1 Corinthians it comes directly after it, while in Mark it is directly before. Both are highly concerned with the Last/Lord's Supper and proper participation, but Paul's is a warning that follows the account, while in Mark it precedes it.

The Quest for Mark's Sources

Theme

Both deal with unworthiness and condemnation. This section of 1 Corinthians deals with the consequences of partaking in the Lord's Supper in an unworthy manner and the consequences are condemnation. Paul believes this unworthy partaking has resulted in many of the Corinthian community becoming ill and dying and that if they were to be correct in their participation they would not be condemned. Essentially the condemnation is illness and death for not participating in the Lord's Supper in the correct manner. In the corresponding section in Mark, namely Mark 14:17–21, there is also condemnation. Here, Jesus reveals to his disciples that one of them will betray him and he says that for that person it would have been better if he had never been born. Condemnations do not get more severe than this and, although it is not explicitly stated, it can be said that Judas is not partaking in this Passover/Eucharist in the proper manner as he is there knowing that he is the betrayer and the condemned one. Jesus' condemnation is much more severe than the condemnation of the Corinthians by Paul and essentially amplifies it so that the condemned person will not just suffer death but that it would be better for that person to have never been born. The condemnation is so severe that non-existence is better.

The motif of self-examination and testing is also present in both. Paul asks the Corinthians to examine themselves before they participate in the Lord's Supper so that they do not participate in an unworthy manner. In Mark, Jesus reveals that one of the twelve will betray him. The effect of this is that the disciples begin to question themselves and ask Jesus individually "Is it I?" They are essentially examining themselves in order to find out if they might be the betrayer. It is interesting that in both 1 Corinthians and Mark, there is self-examination and questioning connected so closely with the Eucharist/Lord's Supper and condemnation.

Both texts deal with the theme of judgement. Paul welcomes judgement by the Lord as a form of discipline to avoid condemnation. Jesus also judges the betrayer and condemns him. The focus of each text is different here. Paul's focus is firmly placed on people who are abusing the Lord's Supper while Mark is focused on the individual betrayer.

Comparison and Analysis of 1 Corinthians 11:2–34 and Mark 14:1–25

Action/Plot and Order

In terms of action/plot, the differing genres preclude much similarity. Some parallels, however, need to be noted. The major themes happen in the same basic order. The unworthy participant/participants theme leads to a self questioning which, in turn, leads to a judgement. The essential elements are the same and occur in the same order.

Vocabulary

In terms of vocabulary there is little to link these two sections beyond ἐσθίω, ἔρχομαι, and ἄνθρωπος. The verb ἐσθίω is to be expected as both sections are set within the context of a meal.

Completeness

First Corinthians 11:27–34 consists of three major elements: unworthy eating, self-examination and judgement. All of these find a parallel within Mark 14:17–21.

Assessment and Conclusion

The data collected can be summarized as follows:
- Both texts are set within the context of meal close to a description of the Last Supper.
- Both contain the motif of unworthy participation.
- Both contain an element of self-examination as a result of this unworthy participation.
- Both lead to an ending judgement.
- Both share the vocabulary ἐσθίω, ἔρχομαι, and ἄνθρωπος.

Thematically there are a lot of parallels. Both texts share an affinity that comes within the context of a much larger chain of similarities. Along with these similarities to 1 Cor 11:27–34 is a larger reliance on Old Testament texts which leads Mark to cast Jesus in the role of the suffering servant and righteous sufferer and Judas as the "bosom friend." Underneath all this, however, is the Markan narrative of the life and ministry of Jesus of

Nazareth. It is within this context that the similarities noted above need to be understood.

ASSESSING THE EVIDENCE: THE CRITERIA FOR JUDGING LITERARY DEPENDENCE

External Criteria

The external criteria have not changed and do not need to be restated.

Internal Criteria

1. Similarities of context, theme, action/plot, order and completeness.

   Context—The contexts of both sections analyzed are similar in that they both come at the beginning of larger sections towards the end of each document ending with a discussion/depiction of the resurrection.

   Theme—Throughout the analysis a plethora of shared themes arose. The first was a focus on the controversial actions of women. Paul is discussing the conduct of women and their head coverings during prayer while Mark narrates the anointing of Jesus' head by a woman. The presence of women is not remarkable and the connection to the human head in both is also not remarkable as Mark's scene is modelled on Old Testament anointing scenes. However, it was the theme of women and people being contentious/angry over their actions that made the parallel striking. Both sections also appeal beyond their immediate context.

   The theme of coming together to eat also ran through the texts. Paul instructs the Corinthians on how they should come together to eat the Lord's Supper while in Mark, Jesus instructs the disciples how to prepare for the Passover. Later in both texts there are unworthy participants, self-examination, condemnations and judgments.

   In the accounts of the Last Supper/Eucharist the elements of bread, wine, body, blood and covenant are all present. The closeness of the accounts is reinforced by the surrounding thematic links.

   Action/Plot—In terms of action and plot, the most striking parallels come in the depiction of the Last Supper/Eucharist but they are part of a larger progression that progresses from the beginning of each section.

Comparison and Analysis of 1 Corinthians 11:2–34 and Mark 14:1–25

Women initially plan in important role in both, and are connected to the human head and angry/contentious people. A contrasting meal setting comes next with divisions in Corinth and harmony in Mark. In both Eucharist scenes the action is mirrored, Jesus takes the bread, blesses/ gives thanks, equates bread with body, takes the cup, equates blood with covenant, Paul and Jesus look forward to the eschatological future. Paul finally moves on to discuss the conduct of people at the Lord's Supper and here, as in Mark, unworthy participants are present and are judged and condemned. The common plot points have often been ascribed to a common source but when taken into consideration with surrounding context this option becomes increasingly unlikely.

Order—The overall series of parallels also share a rough order. The portrayal of women and contentious/angry people is followed by division/ unity, Eucharist and unworthy participants. These last two are reversed in Mark with Eucharist coming last. The internal order of the Eucharist scenes are also similar.

Completeness—Is every major aspect of 1 Cor 11:2–34 matched in Mark 14:1–25? Many aspects are, including the many themes noted. Remembrance, which appears to be missing from Mark's Eucharistic account, is found in the anointing scene. Elements such as the head coverings of women are not entirely matched in Mark, but the precise meaning of 1 Corinthians remains elusive.

2. Common Vocabulary—In most cases the vocabulary was common yet in many cases was connected to the prevailing themes. Some vocabulary deserves note. In 1 Cor 11:16 and Mark 14:4 both use similar phrasing in connection with angry and contentious people. First Corinthians 11:16 in part reads: δέ τις δοκεῖ φιλόνεικος εἶναι. Mark 14:4, in a similar fashion, reads: ἦσαν δέ τινες ἀγανακτοῦντες. Although they are common words they are, nevertheless, clustered around rare words about contentious/ angry people.

   The vocabulary shared in the Eucharist accounts was substantial and goes beyond the possibilities of coincidence. The shared themes, action/ plot and order along with the shared vocabulary make dependence in one form or another highly likely.

3. Literary convention(s) being employed—level of text absorption—The similarities between these texts could be explained by simple text absorption. If 1 Corinthians is a source here then plot points have been generally retained and kept in the same order. There are also contrasts. There is a hint of dispersion in the moving of the remembrance from the

context of the Eucharist to the anointing in Mark which may serve the purpose of foreshadowing what is to come.

In terms of the level of text absorption, there is not one clear answer. In regards to the Eucharist texts themselves there is clearly a close connection and this is consistent with paraphrase and possibly reference. Heuristic imitation is also a possibility here as the usage is not slavish as with sacramental imitation but rather shows some level of change to suit its new context. However, these levels of text absorption cannot be claimed for the other sections that have been analyzed here where transformative allusion, eclectic and possibly dialectical imitation remain the most obvious possibilities.

4. Intelligibility/Interpretability of the differences—Paul has a transitioning sentence to change to a narrative form 1 Cor 11:23). Mark, understandably, does not retain this as he is already writing a narrative and has no need of this transitional sentence. The two texts also have a slightly different focus which results in certain differences. Paul is addressing circumstances in Corinth where people are abusing the Lord's Supper. Therefore, Paul's focus is on the remembrance aspect and the correct way of doing this. For Mark, this is not the case. While it is undoubtedly important and reflects its significance in the early church it is more concerned with the coming events of Jesus' arrest, trial and death. The Eucharist is a pivotal moment of calm before the climax of the gospel. Both look to the future but in different ways.

Many of the differences in the surrounding context of the Eucharist scene are intelligible through the use of different genres. Paul's letter flows differently to Mark's narrative. Thus, when Paul lapses into narrative, closer similarities are found. Also, many other sources present themselves in Mark, some appearing to be major sources which influence the text in a greater way than in 1 Corinthians.

Probing Criteria

1. Strong and weak connections—Some connections, such as the head coverings of women in 1 Corinthians and Jesus' head being covered by oil in Mark, are weak. These connections are only supporting evidence in a larger chain of similarities that leads up to the Eucharistic scenes. Unlike 1 Cor 1–2 where little could be used as supporting evidence, the weaker connections here take on more importance because of the presence of strong connections. The Eucharist scenes, while containing differences,

Comparison and Analysis of 1 Corinthians 11:2–34 and Mark 14:1–25

share many important pieces of vocabulary and plot and many of the differences noted are intelligible because of the presence of other sources and Mark's narrative purpose. The setting, common action/plot and order and shared vocabulary in the Eucharist scenes constitute strong connections. The weaker connections in the surrounding sections can be used as supporting evidence to the stronger connections but cannot, on their own, warrant a case for literary dependence.

2. Similarities that may be due to a common tradition—There is a possibility that has been raised by some scholars, namely that a common tradition underlies both versions. This possibility relies on hypothetical written and oral traditions which, unless found, can never really be proven to have existed and cannot be tested. Working with two extant texts provides a much stronger base for theories of gospel origins.

    The argument of a liturgical source for Mark is that the tradition reflects the form of the Eucharist as used by Mark's own community. This is a very specific historical claim. Liturgical traditions are neither verifiable nor falsifiable; they exist in a methodological limbo. While it is appealing, the temptation to evoke these hypothetical traditions is fraught with problems. How can a liturgical tradition be compared to 1 Corinthians as a source for Mark? In short, it cannot. In favor of rejecting the notion of a liturgical source, written or oral, comes from the texts surrounding the Eucharist. While the Eucharist texts are close, it is the connections between Mark and 1 Corinthians in these surrounding texts that lead to this conclusion. For example, preceding the Eucharist in both texts are scenes involving angry and contentious people, judgment and condemnation. As has also been seen, there are many shared themes, elements of action and plot and some shared vocabulary. When assessed along with the level of similarity in the Eucharist scenes, a liturgical source seems all the more unlikely. The possibility of a common liturgical tradition is not a satisfying one when considering the existence of a model for Mark in 1 Corinthians.

3. Similarities that may be due to a general familiarity of the source text—The shared aspects of plot, correct order, shared themes, contexts and vocabulary point to a connection that is deeper than one of a general familiarity. The evidence presented indicates that one text was based closely on the other, particularly in reference to the Eucharist account.

4. Redundancy—Does another source account for the data found here? No other extant literary source accounts for the data in Mark 14:22–25 more than 1 Cor 11:23–26. Elements of Exodus can be seen but this does not

account for the data in a more satisfactory manner. No other text can be shown to be as close to Mark here without appealing to traditions which are hypothetical and unnecessary.

In the surrounding contexts of the Eucharistic accounts a web of allusions to other texts can be seen. Sometimes these come through in a stronger manner than the parallels to 1 Corinthians. In one instance other sources may appear to make 1 Corinthians redundant and this is the parallel of women and head coverings. While women and the covering of the human head appear in both, the Markan scene is clearly modelled on Old Testament anointing scenes as indicated. However, some elements including the angry/contentious people are not accounted for by these Old Testament texts.

CONCLUSION

Two of the core parts of 1 Corinthians and Mark have been taken and compared and it has been seen how Mark may have taken Paul's version of the inauguration of the Eucharist and transformed it for his own purposes. Out of all the texts which have been analyzed these two are the most similar and recount the same event and share the same plot, order or events and theme as well as vocabulary. Both look to the eschatological future and see the Eucharist as being part of larger and unfolding events. While Mark's text contains some differences, the core of the story is very similar to 1 Corinthians. The connections in the surrounding contexts of these texts show that a common tradition, written or oral, is not a sufficient hypothesis. The two earliest extant forms of the Eucharist come from 1 Corinthians and Mark and they are similar. Luke may provide more striking parallels but this does not mean Markan dependence is not valid. The possibility of Lukan dependence on 1 Corinthians is one that cannot be explored here but the closer similarities certainly fit in with how Luke treats his sources such as Mark, which in many places is largely unchanged. Here rather, there is an instance where it can be said with a huge degree of certainty that Mark is using 1 Corinthians as a literary source.

The larger contexts of the Eucharist texts indicate further that the parallels found within the Eucharist accounts are consistent with larger literary borrowing. The surrounding contexts also helped to make intelligible certain differences between the two texts. In particular, it was seen how Mark's account of the reference to remembrance earlier in chapter 14

Comparison and Analysis of 1 Corinthians 11:2–34 and Mark 14:1–25

makes sense as a way to prefigure coming events. The surrounding context provides supporting evidence to the connection of the Eucharist accounts and, therefore, helps to further a case for literary dependence.

Assessment and Conclusion

Following the analysis of portions of 1 Corinthians and Mark, many similarities between the two texts have been noted and explored. What can be concluded from this information and where can scholarship move from here?

Scholars from Volkmar to Dykstra have noted certain similarities between the Gospel of Mark and the letters of Paul. The question was never fully explored and it has never been fully investigated. This study represents an attempt at a large-scale literary analysis of selected texts from one of Paul's letters and the Gospel of Mark.

Given this recurring perception that the Gospel of Mark and the letters of Paul may be connected, the question has to be asked, what kind of connection could this be? This present study has been concerned with exploring whether or not this connection was literary in nature. The dominant view of Mark in the past one hundred years was that Mark was "*Unliterarisch*," as Bultmann termed it.[1] However, as was seen throughout this study, Mark has been increasingly viewed as a capable author who was at home in the literary world and this included the use of written sources. However, while sources remained elusive, a connection to Paul persisted. It is well known that Matthew and Luke could use written sources as their use of Mark indicated. Mark's only extant written sources appeared, for many years, to be the Jewish Scriptures. Throughout this investigation many connections to the Old Testament were seen, especially to the Elijah-Elisha narrative in 1 and 2 Kings. These Old Testament texts were woven into the fabric of the gospel and transformed. This was consistent with Greco-Roman and Jewish methods of text absorption.

---

1. Bultmann, *History*, 7.

Assessment and Conclusion

A central question asked was did Mark use older Christian writings just as he had used Jewish writings? Was 1 Corinthians one of these sources? It was seen, based on previous scholarly work that these questions needed to be answered. An obvious place to start this investigation was at the beginning of the texts by comparing Mark 1:1–28 to 1 Cor 1–2. The initial impression was discouraging. Yet, when analyzing the texts in close detail certain parallels began to appear and a chain of similarities emerged. Of the seven sections that form 1 Cor 1–2, each one is matched, in some way, by one of the seven sections of Mark 1:1–28.

The two texts were compared to each other on various levels, including context, theme, action/plot and order, completeness and vocabulary. Vocabulary links were generally strongest with each text's opposite number. For example, Paul's baptism text (1 Cor 1:14–17) and Mark's baptism text (Mark 1:4–8) shared vocabulary and such links also extended to nearby texts. However, none of the vocabulary links found in these two sections were significant enough on their own to warrant a case for literary dependence. Once the texts had been compared, the similarities found were analyzed through the criteria for judging literary dependence which served the purpose of making sure that nothing could be claimed without reasonable evidence.

The connections were not always immediately obvious and some were indeed stronger than others. For example, the accounts of the testing of the calls—the Corinthian's examination of their call (1 Cor 1:26–31), and Satan's examining or tempting of Jesus just after his call (Mark 1:12–13) offered no shared vocabulary, but Mark's verbal combination of *Satan* and *tempting* is found nowhere else in the entire Greek Bible except in 1 Cor 7:5, so even in the temptation narrative, Mark has a vocabulary link to 1 Corinthians through another portion of the text. The strongest similarities are as follows:

- The common usage of the verb καταρτίζω (to mend). This verb, as was seen, is uncommon in the LXX and the New Testament.

- The common chain of themes includes baptism, revelation, unity, displays of power, teaching and the spiritual call. Certain situations in Mark present a contrast to that in Corinth. Mark often presents an ideal situation, positivizing the situation in Corinth. The purpose of this could be pedagogical in nature. Mark is showing how Christians should act, rather than how they are acting. This was seen clearly when dealing with the theme of unity in 1 Cor 1:10–13 and Mark 1:16–20.

- The shared three-part structure of 1 Cor 2 and Mark 1:21-28 based around preaching, doomed ruler/spirits, mystery and the Spirit. This tied these two sub-units together creating stark parallels.

Each subsection of Mark analyzed was found to have some affinity with a section of 1 Corinthians creating a chain of similarities and a certain completeness. However, ambiguity is left as this chain was largely weak in nature and cannot support a case for literary dependence. This needs to be viewed against the background of Mark's larger web of sources. A strong reliance on 1 and 2 Kings was noted and this formed Mark's major source in many instances. First Corinthians, if indeed a source here, is a lesser source. The similarities noted shared some consistency with methods of text absorption such as distillation, dispersion, positivization and *contaminatio*. Contrasting elements were also found. These contrasting elements present a problem as it makes differences evidence as well as similarities and this can create false results as it means that nothing can be discounted. Differences are not included as evidence for dependence on their own but rather a specific kind of difference. When the action/plot of 1 Corinthians is, seemingly, reversed in Mark, it is noted as possibly being deliberate in nature. This is specific in nature and is not a matter of using anything as evidence.

The differences between the two texts were intelligible for many reasons. Firstly, Mark is dependent on many Old Testament texts which were his primary sources. Secondly, the two texts are written in distinct genres. Paul is writing a letter while Mark is writing in narrative prose. Thirdly, Mark has specific purposes that do not always fit in with Paul's. Finally and most importantly, Mark is narrating the life of Jesus and this is the driving force behind the text.

Following the ambiguity of the evidence from the analysis of 1 Cor 1-2 and Mark 1:1-28 a second area was analyzed which was 1 Cor 5 and Mark 6:14-29. These texts were chosen for analysis because of a similar situation in both, namely a man living with someone prohibited by Jewish Law. There were many elements throughout the analysis which indicated literary dependence.

- Both texts revolved around a man who was living with a woman which Jewish Law forbids him from living with. Levitical laws lie behind both texts, yet do not account for all of the similarities.
- There is a similar progression in both texts where the actions of the sexually immoral person is condemned, the removal or call for removal of a

person occurs in both, the destruction of the flesh is in both, and Satan is mentioned in 1 Cor 5:5 while satanic characters appear in Mark.

While there was little in terms of vocabulary to suggest a literary connection, the thematic similarities and correlation of plot was strong. *Varatio*, contemporization and *contaminatio* are all possibly being used here by Mark.

The final area analyzed was 1 Cor 11:2–34 and Mark 14:1–25. These texts were chosen because contained in them are the two earliest extant accounts of the Last Supper/Eucharist. The main points that can contribute to a case of literary dependence are as follows:

- The theme of coming together to eat ran throughout the texts. Paul instructs the Corinthians on how they should come together to eat the Lord's Supper while in Mark, Jesus instructs the disciples how to prepare for the Passover. The Last Supper/Eucharist is then depicted in both. Later in both texts, there are unworthy participants, self-examination, condemnations and judgements. While the context of the meal is not significant itself, when considered part of a large chain of similarities, the connections cannot be ignored.

- From the beginning of each section there is a common sequence of action/plot in roughly the same order. Women initially play an important role in both and are connected to the human head and angry/contentious people. A contrasting meal setting comes next with divisions in Corinth and harmony in Mark. In both Eucharist scenes this action is mirrored. Jesus takes the bread, blesses/gives thanks, equates bread with body, takes the cup, equates blood with covenant, Paul and Jesus look forward to the eschatological future. Paul finally moves on to discuss the conduct of people at the Lord's Supper and here, as in Mark, unworthy participants are present and are judged and condemned.

- In 1 Cor 11:16 and Mark 14:4 both use similar phrasing in connection with angry and contentious people.

- The shared vocabulary in the Eucharistic scenes is significant. This is combined with a similar plot, order and larger context.

The similarities between the Eucharistic scenes are often ascribed to the presence of a liturgical tradition. However, when the larger chain of similarities is taken into account then this no longer becomes a viable hypothesis. Liturgical traditions are, ultimately, hypothetical and caught in a methodological limbo where it cannot be either verified or falsified. After weighing up the evidence contained in the Eucharistic texts and in the surrounding texts the only logical solution is that Mark is dependent upon 1 Corinthians. This again must be viewed against the backdrop of Mark's dependence upon Old Testament texts which really comes to the fore here where the reader is presented with a complex web of allusions which made redundant some of the similarities noted. However, it is in Mark 14:22–25 that 1 Corinthians takes precedence above all other sources. As with 1 Cor 1–2 and Mark 1:1–28 the similarities noted were consistent with methods of text absorption such as distillation, dispersion, positivization and *contaminatio*. Here too, contrasting elements were found.

Overall, what can be said about the exploration between Mark and 1 Corinthians? This was an experimental investigation that did not expect to stumble across an easy answer, as, if it were obvious, it would already be known. However, some answers have been revealed through analysis of the text. Following this analysis it can be said that some of the similarities noted between Mark and 1 Corinthians are consistent with literary dependence. Many weak connections were noted and these cannot contribute to a case for literary dependence but those similarities listed above indicate a relationship. The analysis revealed that this cannot be ascribed to a common tradition or that Mark was merely working within a Pauline sphere of influence but rather that 1 Corinthians was not Mark's primary source but rather one of many and one that is not immediately apparent through a simple reading of the text.

If it can be established that there is a literary link between these two texts, then to what level is Mark dependent on 1 Corinthians? In terms of 1 Cor 1–2 and Mark 1:1–28 the level of text absorption does not appear to fit into any one category. What was seen throughout were similarities that were consistent with elements of allusion and in particular transforming allusion. Elements of Mark's text presented a contrast to the situation Paul describes in Corinth, a contrast which conforms to transforming allusion. This is also consistent with dialectical imitation where a contrast is formed with the source text within its new literary context. The contrasts between Mark and 1 Corinthians seem to indicate the possibility as the texts are complementary. Mark's reliance on multiple sources is consistent with eclectic imitation where not one source is given primary significance but rather multiple sources are mingled together. However, allusion does not completely explain what has been noted, as allusions usually give textual indicators of the presence of a source. The similarities noted in this present study have been very subtle in nature. Therefore, with regards to 1 Cor 1–2 and Mark 1:1–28, a literary connection could not be shown with confidence and while there was some consistency with ancient literary techniques, the absence of overt literary markers damages any case for dependence.

However, when looking at 1 Cor 5 and Mark 6:14–29, many stronger parallels were noted and both authors presented very similar situations. *Varatio*, contemporization, and *contaminatio* were all noted and these techniques appear to be working in the context of conforming allusion and eclectic imitation. The technique of *contaminatio*, in particular, is interesting as Mark consistently weaves together multiple sources in the composition of the gospel.

In regard to 1 Cor 11:2–34 and Mark 14:1–25 the issue is somewhat more complex as the similarities between the two texts are not consistent and are stronger in some areas of the text. The Eucharist accounts presented the strongest similarities and these were consistent with paraphrase and possibly reference. Heuristic imitation is also a possibility here as the usage is not slavish, as with sacramental imitation, but rather shows some level of change to suit its new context.

The description of the Last Supper in 1 Cor 11:23–26 presented Mark with a rare opportunity in Pauline literature of employing a more overt narrative form. Therefore, the similarities found here are different to those found in other places. With the volume of similarities between the two texts, the methods used and the consistency with certain levels of textual absorption, it can be concluded that there is a literary relationship between 1 Corinthians and Mark and that 1 Corinthians represents one component of the Gospel of Mark although this is not always overt in nature.

However, this study analyzed only one of Paul's letters, and not the entire document. To fully analyze a complete letter was simply too large for the scope of this investigation. Future areas of research would need to focus on other parts of 1 Corinthians and other letters in the Pauline corpus in order to see the full extent of the literary connection to Mark. Other letters may yield greater results and some may be fruitless. However, this first probing into the literary connection between Mark and Paul has been largely positive and shows that further investigation is required.

Bibliography

ANCIENT SOURCES

Ante-Nicene Fathers: Apostolic Fathers, Justin Martyr and Irenaeus. Edited by A. Roberts, and J. Donaldson. Peabody, MA: Hendrickson, 1999.

Ante-Nicene Fathers: Gospel of Peter, Diatessaron, Testament of Abraham, Epistles of Clement, Origen, Miscellaneous Works. Edited by A. Menzies. Peabody, MA: Hendrickson, 1999.

Ante-Nicene Fathers: Hippolytus, Cyprian, Caius, Novatian. Edited by A. Roberts and J. Donaldson. Peabody, MA: Hendrickson, 1999.

Apollonius of Rhodes. *Argonautica*. Translated by William H. Race. LCL 1. Cambridge: Harvard University Press, 2008.

Cicero. *De Finibus*. Translated by H. Rackham. LCL 40. Cambridge: Harvard University Press, 1914.

———. *De Oratore*. Translated by E. W. Sutton and H. Rackham. 2 vols. LCL 348–49. Cambridge: Harvard University Press, 1942.

———. *De Inventione, De Optimo Genere Oratorum*. Translated by Harry M. Hubbell. LCL 386. Cambridge: Harvard University Press, 1976.

Dionysius of Halicarnassus. *Critical Essays*. 2 vols. Translated by S. Usher. LCL 465–66. Cambridge: Harvard University Press, 1985.

Greek-English New Testament. Edited by B. Aland and K. Aland. Nestle-Aland 9th ed. Stuttgart: German Bible Society, 2005.

The Greek New Testament. Edited by K. Aland, et al. UBS 3rd ed. Stuttgart: German Bible Society, 1983.

Herodotus. *The Persian Wars*. Translated by A. D. Godley. 4 vols. LCL 117–20. Cambridge: Harvard University Press, 2004.

Homer. *Iliad*. Translated by Richmond Lattimore. Chicago: University of Chicago Press, 1951.

———. *Odyssey*. Translated by Richmond Lattimore. New York: Harper Collins, 1967.

Horace. *Satires, Epistles and Ars Poetica*. Translated by H. R. Fairclough. LCL 194. Cambridge: Harvard University Press, 1926.

Isocrates. *On the Peace, Areopagiticus, Against the Sophists, Antidosis and Panathenaicus*. Translated by G. Norlin. LCL 229. Cambridge: Harvard University Press, 1929.

Lucan. *The Civil War*. Translated by James Duff. LCL 220. Cambridge: Harvard University Press, 1988.

Bibliography

Nicene and Post-Nicene Fathers, First Series: John Chrysostom, Homilies on the Gospel of Saint Matthew. Edited by P. Schaff. Peabody, MA: Hendrickson, 1999.
Nicene and Post-Nicene Fathers, Second Series: Eusebius. Edited by P. Schaff, and H. Wace. Peabody, MA: Hendrickson, 1999.
Nicene and Post-Nicene Fathers, Second Series: Jerome. Edited by P. Schaff, and H. Wace. Peabody, MA: Hendrickson, 1999.
Plutarch. *Lives: Pericles and Fabius Maximus, Nicias and Crassus.* Translated by Bernadette Perrin. LCL 65. Cambridge: Harvard University Press, 2001.
Quintilian. *The Orator's Education.* Translated by H. E. Butler. 5 vols. LCL 124–27 and 494. Cambridge: Harvard University Press, 1920.
Septuagint with Apocrypha. Edited by L. C. L. Brenton. Peabody, MA: Hendrickson, 1986.
Virgil. *Aeneid.* Translated by Allen Mandelbaum. Berkeley: University of California Press, 1982.

SECONDARY LITERATURE

Achtemeier, P. J. *Mark.* 2nd ed. Proclamation Commentaries. Philadelphia: Fortress, 1986.
Alexander, P. S. "Retelling the Old Testament." In *It Is Written: Scripture Citing Scripture* edited by D. A. Carson and H. G. M. Williamson, 99–121. Cambridge: Cambridge University Press, 1988.
Allison, Dale C. *The Intertextual Jesus: Scripture in Q.* Harrisburg, PA: Trinity, 2000.
Bacon, B. W. *The Gospel of Mark: Its Composition and Date.* New Haven, CT: Yale University Press, 1925.
Baird, William. *History of New Testament Research: Volume 2: From Jonathan Edwards to Rudolph Bultmann.* Minneapolis: Fortress, 2003.
Barrett, C. K. *The First Epistle to the Corinthians,* 2nd ed. BNTC. London: Adam & Charles Black, 1971.
Baur, F. C. *Kritische Untersuchungen über die kanonischen Evengalien, ihr Verhältniss zu einander, ihren Charakter und Ursprung.* Tübingen: L. F. Fues, 1847.
Becker, Eve-Marie, et al. "Earliest Christian *Literary Activity*: Investigating Authors, Genres and Audiences in Paul and Mark." In *Mark and Paul: Comparative Essays Part II: For and Against Pauline Influence on Mark,* edited by Eve-Marie Becker et al., 87–105. BZNW 199. Berlin: de Gruyter, 2014.
———. *Mark and Paul: Comparative Essays Part II: For and Against Pauline Influence on Mark.* BZNW 199. Berlin: de Gruyter, 2014.
Betz, H. D. "Paul." In *ABD* 5:186–201.
Bird, Michael F., and Joel Willits. "Mark: Interpreter of Peter and Disciple of Paul." In *Paul and the Gospels: Christologies Conflicts and Convergences,* edited by Michael F. Bird and Joel Willits, 30–61. LNTS 411. London: T. & T. Clark, 2011.
———. *Paul and the Gospels: Christologies Conflicts and Convergences.* LNTS 411. London: T. & T. Clark, 2011.
Black, C. Clifton. *Mark: Images of an Apostolic Interpreter.* South Carolina: University of South Carolina Press, 1994.
Bowra, C. M. "Aeneas and the Stoic Ideal." In *Virgil: Critical Assessments of Classical Authors,* edited by Philip Hardie, 204–17. 4 vols. New York: Routledge, 1999.
———. *Heroic Poetry.* London: Macmillan, 1952.

Bibliography

Brodie, Thomas L. *The Birthing of the New Testament.* New Testament Monographs 1. Sheffield: Sheffield Phoenix, 2004.

———. *Genesis as Dialogue.* Oxford: Oxford University Press, 2001.

———. *The Quest for the Origins of John's Gospel.* Oxford: Oxford University Press, 1993.

Brooke, George J. "The Rewritten Law, Prophets and Psalms: Issues for Understanding the Text of the Bible." In *The Bible as Book: The Hebrew Bible and the Judean Desert Discoveries,* edited by Edward D. Herbert and Emanuel Tov, 31–40. London: British Library and New Castle, 2002.

Bultmann, Rudolph. *History of the Synoptic Tradition.* Translated by John Marsh. New York: Harper and Row, 1963.

Burchard, Christoph. "The Importance of Joseph and Aseneth for the Study of the New Testament: A General Survey and a Fresh Look at the Lord's Supper." *NTS* 33 (1987) 102–34.

Chesnutt, R. D. *From Death to Life: Conversion in Joseph and Aseneth.* Sheffield: Sheffield Academic, 1995.

Ciampa, Roy E., and Brian S. Rosner. *The First Letter to the Corinthians.* Grand Rapids: Eerdmans, 2010.

Clausen, W. V. *Virgil's Aeneid and the Tradition of Hellenistic Poetry.* Berkeley and London: University of California Press, 1987.

Collins, Adela Yarbro. *Mark.* Hermeneia. Minneapolis: Fortress, 2007.

Collins, R. F. *First Corinthians.* Collegeville, MN: Liturgical, 1999.

Conte, G. B. *Genres and Readers: Lucretius, Love, Elegy, Pliny's Encyclopaedia.* Translated by G. W. Mast. Baltimore: John Hopkins OB, 1994.

———. *The Rhetoric of Imitation: Genre and Poetic Memory in Virgil and Other Latin Poets.* Translated by Charles Segal. Ithica, NY: Cornell University Press, 1996.

Conzelmann, Hans. *1 Corinthians.* Hermeneia. Philadelphia: Fortress, 1975.

Crawford, Sidnie White. *Rewriting Scripture in Second Temple Times.* Grand Rapids: Eerdmans, 2008.

Crossan, J. D. *Four Other Gospels: Shadows on the Contours of Canon.* New York. Harper & Row, 1985.

———. "Mark and the Relatives of Jesus." *NovT* 15 (1973) 81–113.

Crossley, James G. *The Date of the Mark's Gospel: Insight from the Law in Earliest Christianity.* JSNTSup 266. Edinburgh: T. & T. Clark, 2004.

———. "Mark, Paul and the Question of Influences." In *Paul and the Gospels: Christologies Conflicts and Convergences,* edited by Michael F. Bird and Joel Willits, 10–29. LNTS 411. London: T. & T. Clark, 2011.

Derrenbacker, Robert A. *Ancient Compositional Practices and the Synoptic Problem.* Leuven: Leuven University Press, 2005.

Dimmant, Devorah. "Use and Interpretation of Mikra in the Apocrrpha and Pseudepigrapha." In *Mikra: Text, Translation, Reading and Interpretation of the Hebrew Bible in Ancient Judaism and Early Christianity,* edited by M. J. Mulder and H. Sysling, 379–419. CRINT II 1. Philadelphia: Fortress, 1988.

Dixon, E. P. "Descending Spirit and Descending Gods: A "Greek" Interpretation of the Spirit's "Descending as a Dove" in Mark 1:10." *JBL* 128 (2009) 759–80.

Dochhorn, J. "Man and the Son of Man in Mark 2:27–28: An Exegesis of Mark 2:23–28 Focussing on the Christological Discourse in Mark 2:27–28 with an Epilogue Concerning Pauline Parallels." In *Mark and Paul: Comparative Essays Part II: For and Against Pauline Influence on Mark*, edited by Eve-Marie Becker et al., 147–68. BZNW 199. Berlin: de Gruyter, 2014.

Dowd, Sharyn. *Reading Mark*. Macon: Smyth & Helwys, 2000.

Dykstra, Tom. *Mark Canonizer of Paul: A New Look at Intertextuality in Mark's Gospel*. Worcester, MA: Ocabs, 2012.

Fenton, J. C. "Mark and Paul." In *Studies in the Gospels: Essays in Memory of R. H. Lightfoot*, edited by D. E. Nineham, 89–112. Oxford: Basil Blackwell, 1957.

Finkelpearl, E. "Pagan Traditions of Intertextuality in the Roman World." In *Mimesis and Intertextuality in Antiquity and Christianity*, edited by Dennis R. MacDonald, 78–90. Harrisburg, PA: Trinity International, 2001.

Fishbane, Michael. *Biblical Interpretation in Ancient Israel*. Oxford: Clarendon, 1985.

Fiske, G. C. *Lucilius and Horace: A Study in the Classical Theory of Imitation*. Reprint. Westport, CT: Greenwood, 1971.

Fitzmyer, J. A. *First Corinthians*. AB 32. New Haven: Yale University Press, 2008.

———. "The Letter to the Romans." In *JBC* 2:291–331.

Fuchs, A. "Die Entwicklung der Beelzebulkontroverse bei den Synoptikern. Traditionsgeschichtliche und redaktionsgeschichtliche Untersuchungen von Mk 3:22–27 und Parallelen, verbunden mit der Rückfrage nach Jesus." SNTSU 5 (1980) 139–49.

Fuller, R. H. "Baur Versus Hildenfeld: A Forgotten Chapter in the Debate on the Synoptic Problem." *NTS* 24 (1978) 355–70.

Goulder, Michael D. "A Pauline in Jacobite Church." In *The Four Gospels*, 3 vols., edited by F. Van Segbroeck et al., 859–76. Leuven: Leuven University Press, 1992.

Gransden, K. W. *Virgil—The Aeneid*. 4th ed. Cambridge: Cambridge University Press, 1999.

Greene, Thomas M. *The Descent From Heaven: A Study in Epic Continuity*. New Haven, CT: Yale University Press, 1963.

———. *The Light in Troy: Imitation and Discovery in Renaissance Poetry*. New Haven, CT: Yale University Press, 1982.

Harman, G.H. and S. Budick. *Midrash and Literature*. New Haven, CT: Yale University Press, 1986.

Hays, Richard B. *Echoes of Scripture in the Letters of Paul*. New Haven, CT: Yale University Press, 1989.

———. *First Corinthians*. Louisville: John Knox, 1997.

Hengel, Martin. *Jews, Greeks and Barbarians: Aspects of Hellenization of Judaism in the pre-Christian Period*. Philadelphia: Fortress, 1980.

———. *Studies in the Gospel of Mark*. Eugene, OR: Wipf and Stock, 1985.

Hinds, Stephen. *Allusion and Intertext: Dynamics of Appropriation in Roman Poetry*. Cambridge: Cambridge University Press, 1998.

Holtzmann, H. J. *Die synoptischen Evangelien. Ihr Ursprung und geschichtlicher Charakter*. Leipzig: Wilhelm Engelmann, 1863.

Hooker, Morna D. *The Gospel According to St. Mark*. BNTC. Reprint. New York: Continuum, 2003.

Hull, J. M. *Hellenistic Magic and the Synoptic Tradition*. London: SCM, 1974.

Jeremias, Joachim. *The Eucharistic Words of Jesus*. Translated by Norman K. Perrin. Philadelphia: Fortress, 1966.

Kealy, Sean P. *A History of the Interpretation of the Gospel of Mark*. 2 vols. New York: Edwin Mellen, 2007.

Bibliography

Kee, Howard C. *Good News to the Ends of the Earth: The Theology of Act.* London: SCM, 1990.

Kermode, Frank. *The Genesis of Secrecy: On the Interpretation of Narrative.* Cambridge: Harvard University Press, 1979.

Koester, H. "History and Development of Mark's Gospel: From Mark to Secret Mark and "Canonical" Mark." In *Colloquy on New Testament Studies: A Time for Reappraisal and Fresh Approaches,* edited by B. Corley, 35–58. Macon, GA: Mercer, 1983.

Krentz, E. M. "First and Second Epistles to the Thessalonians." In *ABD* 6:515–522.

Lambert, W. G. *Babylonian Wisdom Literature.* Oxford: Clarendon, 1960.

Lane, W. M. *The Gospel of Mark.* NICNT. Grand Rapids: Eerdmans, 1974.

Leon-Dufour, X. *Sharing the Eucharistic Bread: the Witness of the New Testament.* Translated by Matthew J. O'Connell. New York: Paulist, 1987.

Leppä, O. *The Making of Colossians: A Study on the Formation and Purpose of a Deutero-Pauline Letter.* Göttingen: Vandenhoeck & Ruprecht, 2003.

Levine, L. I. *Judaism and Hellenism in Antiquity: Conflict or Confluence?* Peabody, MA: Hendrickson, 1999.

Lietzmann, Hans. *Mass and Lord's Supper.* Translated by Dorothea H. G. Reeve. Leiden: Brill, 1953.

Luce, T. J. *Livy: The Composition of History.* Princeton: Princeton University Press, 1977.

MacDonald, Dennis R. "A Categorization of Antetextuality in the Gospels and Acts: A Case for Luke's Imitation of Plato and Xenephon to Depict Paul as a Christian Socrates." In *The Intertextuality of the Epistles: Explorations of Theory and Practice,* edited by Thomas L. Brodie et al., 211–25. New Testament Monographs 16. Sheffield: Sheffield Phoenix, 2006.

———. *The Homeric Epics and Gospel of Mark.* New Haven, CT: Yale University Press, 2000.

Mackay, L. A. "Achilles as Model for Aeneas." In *Virgil: Critical Assessments of Classical Authors.* 4 vols, edited by P. Hardie, 87–92. London: Routledge, 1999.

Marcus, Joel. *Mark.* 2 vols. AB 27–27A. New York: Doubleday, 2000–2009.

———. "Mark—Interpreter of Paul." *NTS* 46 (2000) 473–87.

———. "Mark—Interpreter of Paul." In *Mark and Paul: Comparative Essays Part II: For and Against Pauline Influence on Mark,* edited by Eve-Marie Becker et al., 29–49. BZNW 199. Berlin: de Gruyter, 2014.

———. *The Way of the Lord: Christological Exegesis of the Old Testament in the Gospel of Mark.* Edinburgh: T. & T. Clark, 1993.

Marshall, I. H. "The Lord's Supper." In *DPL* 569–75.

Martin, Ralph P. *Evangelist and Theologian.* Grand Rapids: Zondervan, 1973.

———. "The Theology of Mark's Gospel." *SwJT* 21 (1978) 23–26.

Marxsen, W. *Mark the Evangelist.* Translated by R. A. Harrisville. Nashville: Abingdon, 1969.

McKeon, R. "Literary Criticism and the Concept of Imitation in Antiquity." *Modern Philology* 34 (1936) 1–35.

Miller, P. A. *Lyric Texts and Lyric Consciousness: The Birth of Genre from Archaic Greece to Augustan Rome.* London: Routledge, 1994.

Murphy-O'Connor, Jerome. "The First Letter to the Corinthians." In *NJBC* 798–815.

Neil, S., and T. Wright, *The Interpretation of The New Testament 1861–1986.* Oxford: Oxford University Press, 1988.

Bibliography

Nelis, D. *Vergil's Aeneid and the Argonautica of Apollonius Rhodius.* Leeds: Francis Cairns, 2001.

Nelligan, Thomas P. Review of *Paul and the Gospels: Christologies Conflicts and Convergences*, by Michael F. Bird and Joel Willits. *RBL* 11 (2012). No pages. Online: http://www.bookreviews.org/pdf/8336_9115.pdf

Neusner, J. *Judaism and the Interpretation of Scripture: Introduction to the Rabbinic Midrash.* Peabody, MA: Hendrickson, 2004.

Noonan-Sabin, M. *The Gospel According to Mark.* New Collegeville Bible Commentary 2. Minneapolis: Liturgical, 2006.

———. *Reopening the Word: Reading Mark as Theology in the Context of Early Judaism.* Oxford: Oxford University Press, 2002.

O'Leary, A. M. *Matthew's Judaization of Mark.* JSNTSup 323. Edinburgh: T. & T. Clark, 2006.

Omerzu, H. "Paul and Mark—Mark and Paul: A Critical Outline of the History of Research." In *Mark and Paul: Comparative Essays Part II: For and Against Pauline Influence on Mark*, edited by Eve-Marie Becker et al., 51–61. BZNW 199. Berlin: de Gruyter, 2014.

Ong, Walter J. *Rhetoric, Romance and Technology.* Ithaca, NY: Cornell University Press, 1971.

Orr W. F., and J. A. Walther, *1 Corinthians.* AB 32. New York: Doubleday, 1976.

O'Toole, Robert F. "Last Supper." In *ABD* 4:234–41.

Perrin, N. *What is Redaction Criticism?* Nashville: Abingdon, 1969.

Porton, G. G. "Midrash." In *ABD* 4:818–22.

———. *Understanding Rabbinic Midrash.* New Jersey: KTAV, 1985.

Quinn, K. *Virgil's Aeneid—A Critical Description.* Ann Arbor: University of Michigan Press, 1968.

Rohde, J. *Rediscovering the Teaching of the Evangelists.* London: Barton, 1968.

Sanders, E. P. "Literary Dependence in Colossians." *JBL* 85 (1966) 28–45.

Sandmel, Samuel "Parallelomania." *JBL* 81 (1962) 1–13.

Schmitals, Walter. "Zur Kritik der Formkritik." In *Paulus, die Evangelien und das Urchristentum: Beiträge von und zu Walter Schmithals. Zu seinem 80. Geburtstag herausgegeben*, edited by Cilliers Breytenbach, 275–313. Leiden: Brill, 2004.

Schussler Fiorenza, E. *In Memory of Her.* London: SCM, 1994.

Seeley, David. "Rulership and Service in Mark 10:41–45." *NovT* 3 (1993) 234–50.

Smith, M. *The Secret Gospel: The Discovery and Interpretation of the Secret Gospel According to Mark.* New York: Harper & Row, 1973.

Stahl, H. P. "Aeneas—An "Un-Heroic" Hero?" *Arethusa* 14 (1981) 157–77.

Stamps, D. L. "The Use of the Old Testament in the New Testament as a Rhetorical Device: A Methodological Proposal." In *Hearing the Old Testament in the New Testament*, edited by S. E. Porter, 9–37. Grand Rapids: Eerdmans, 2006.

Stanley, Christopher D. *Paul and the Language of Scripture: Citation Technique in the Pauline Epistles and Contemporary Literature.* Cambridge: Cambridge University Press, 1992.

Stanton, G. *A Gospel for a New People—Studies in Matthew.* Louisville: Westminster John Knox, 1993.

Stein, R. H. "What is Redaktionsgeschichte?" *JBL* 88 (1969) 45–56.

Steiner, George. *After Babel: Aspects of Language and Translation.* Oxford: Oxford University Press, 1975.

Bibliography

Stern, D. "The Rabbinic Parable and the Narrative of Interpretation." In *The Midrashic Imagination: Jewish Exegesis, Thought, and History*, edited by Michael Fishbane, 78–95. Albany: State University of New York Press, 1993.

Sternberg, M. *The Poetics of Biblical Narrative*. Bloomington: Indiana University Press, 1985.

Strack, H. L. and Günter Stemberger. *Introduction to the Talmud and Midrash*. Translated by Markus Bockmuehl. Minneapolis: Fortress, 1992.

Taylor, Vincent. *The Gospel According to St. Mark*. New York: St. Martin's, 1952.

Telford, William R. "Introduction." In *The Interpretation of Mark*, edited by William R. Telford. Edinburgh: T. & T. Clark, 1995.

———. *Mark*. Sheffield: Sheffield Academic, 1995.

———. *The Theology of the Gospel of Mark*. Cambridge: Cambridge University Press, 1999.

Theissen, Gerd. *The Gospels in Context: Social and Political History in the Synoptic Tradition*. Translated by Linda M. Maloney. Reprint. Edinburgh: T. & T. Clark, 1998.

Thiselton, A. C. *First Epistle to the Corinthians*. Grand Rapids: Eerdmans, 2000.

Thomas, R. F. *Reading Virgil and His Texts: Studies in Intertextuality*. Ann Arbor: University of Michigan Press, 1999.

Thompson, M. B. "The Holy Internet: Communication Between Churches in the First Century Generation." In *The Gospel for All Christians: Rethinking Gospel Audiences*, edited by R. Bauckham, 49–70. Grand Rapids: Eerdmans, 1998.

Tolbert, M. A. *Sowing the Gospel: Mark's World in Literary-Historical Perspective*. Minneapolis: Fortress, 1989.

Trocme, E. *The Formation of the Gospel According to Mark*. Translated by P. Gaugin. London: SPCK, 1975.

Tuckett, C. M. "The Griesbach Hypothesis in the 19th Century." *JSNT* 3 (1979) 29–60.

Van Seters, John. *The Edited Bible*. Winona Lake, IN: Eisenbrauns, 2006.

Vermes, Geza. "Bible Interpretation at Qumran." *ErIsr* 20 (1989): 181–91.

Vig Skoven, Anne. "Mark as Allegorical Rewriting of Paul: Gustav Volkmar's Understanding of the Gospel of Mark." In *Mark and Paul: Comparative Essays Part II: For and Against Pauline Influence on Mark*, edited by Eve-Marie Becker et al., 13–27. BZNW 199. Berlin: de Gruyter, 2014.

Volkmar, Gustav. *Die Evangelien; oder, Marcus und die synopsis der kanonischen und ausserkanonishcen Evangelien nach dem altesten text, mit historisch-exegetischem commentar*. Leipzig: Fues, R. Reisland, 1870.

———. *Die Religion Jesu*. Leipzig: F.U. Brockhaus, 1857.

Werner, M. *Der Einfluss paulinischer Theologie im Markusevangelium*. BZNW I. Giessen: Alfred Töpelmann, 1923.

Wildemann, B. *Das Evangelium als Lehrpoesie. Leben und Wek Gustav Volkmars*. Kontexte, 1. New York: Peter Lang, 1983.

Wilke, C. G. *Der Urevangelist oder exegetisch krilische Untersuchung uber das Verwandtschaftsver haltniss der drei ersten Evangelien*. Dresden: Gerhard Fleischer, 1838.

Williams, R. D. *The Aeneid of Virgil—Books 1–6*. New York: St. Martin's, 1989.

Williamson, Lamar, Jr. *Mark*. Louisville: John Knox, 1983.

Winn, Adam. *Mark and the Elijah-Elisha Narrative*. Eugene, OR: Pickwick, 2010.

———. *The Purpose of Mark's Gospel: An Early Christian response to Roman Imperial Propaganda*. WUNT 245. Tubingen: Mohr Siebeck, 2008.

Bibliography

Wischmeyer, O., et al. *Paul and Mark: Comparative Essays Part I: Two Authors at the Beginning of Christianity.* BZNW 198. Berlin: de Gruyter, 2014.

———. "Romans 1:1–7 and Mark 1:1–3 in Comparison: Two Opening Texts at the Beginning of Early Christian Literature." In *Mark and Paul: Comparative Essays Part II: For and Against Pauline Influence on Mark,* edited by Eve-Marie Becker et al., 121–46. BZNW 199. Berlin: de Gruyter, 2014.

Wrede, W. *The Messianic Secret.* Translated by J. C. G. Greig. London: James Clark, 1971.

Subject Index

Achilleus, 7, 10–12
addition, 7
Aeneas, 7, 10–12
Aeneid, 7, 9–12, 29–30, 64
allusion, 8, 10, 15–16, 18–19, 29–30, 43, 47, 96–97, 99, 110–12, 121–22, 126, 128, 131, 134, 139, 144, 146, 152–53
amplification, 7
Apollonius Rhodius, 8–10, 50, 66
Argonautica, 8–10
Augustine, xiii

baptism, 43, 52–53, 55–59, 67–70, 72, 77–80, 82–83, 85, 87, 94, 99, 149

Cicero, 3
citation, 4, 15, 121
compression/synthesis, 8
contamination/*contaminatio*, 8–10, 77, 96, 110, 112, 150–53
contemporization, 7, 12, 110, 112, 151, 153
correction, 8
criteria for judging literary dependence, xvi, 18–32, 54, 92–98, 109–12, 149, 142–46

demon/demonic/demoniac, 45, 89–91, 105–7
distillation, 13, 15, 77, 84–85, 96, 150, 152
distribution, 8, 96

echo, 5, 15–16, 18–20, 24, 30

elaboration, 7
Elijah-Elisha Narrative, xv, 52, 78, 82, 86, 148
Elijah, 61, 73–74, 78, 82, 86, 102
Elisha, 73–74, 78, 82, 85, 89, 127
emulation, 6
εὐαγγέλιον, 45, 48, 61–64
Eucharist, 39, 43, 50, 53, 106–7, 113–19, 124, 128–37, 140, 142–47, 151, 153
exorcism, 56, 88–90

form criticism, xiii

genre, xiv, 3, 13–14, 29, 50–52, 65, 71, 75, 94, 96–97, 125, 130, 141, 144, 150

Hellenism/Hellenization/Hellenistic, xv, 2, 4, 12, 33, 50–51, 66, 116
Herod, 101–4, 106–11
Herodias, 101–3, 107
Herodotus, 103–104
Homer/Homeric, xvi, 7–12, 22, 29, 50, 66, 69, 117, 126

Iliad, 7, 9–11, 22, 64, 68
imitation, xv, 3–17, 22, 30, 47, 66, 82, 96, 99, 111–12, 144, 152–53
internalization, 7
interpretation, 5–6, 11
intertextuality, 20, 47, 66, 68
inventive imitation, 5–7
Isocrates, 3, 5–6

Subject Index

John the Baptist, 56–59, 61, 63–64, 67, 69–70, 78–79, 101, 103–6, 108, 111
Josephus, 13, 104

Last/Lord's Supper, see Eucharist
liturgical traditions, 53, 115, 137, 145, 151
Livy, 104
Lucan, 29–30

Markan Priority, xiii, 36, 92, 116, 118
Midrash, 4, 13–14
mimesis, see imitation

negativization, 7, 96

Odysseus, 9–11, 117, 122, 128, 134
Odyssey, 9–11, 22, 64, 69, 128, 131, 134
omission, 7, 11
oral tradition, xiii–xiv, 22, 47, 145
Ovid, 69

Papias, 34–35
parallelomania, xiv
Paraphrase, 5–6, 15, 144, 153
Peter/Petrine, 34–36, 45–46, 74
Plutarch, 104
positivization, 7, 96, 150, 152
Priene Inscription, 62, 66

Proto-Luke, 20

Quintilian, 3, 5, 7–8
Qumran, 14, 103
quotation, 8, 15, 62, 66

rabbinic literature, 14
redaction criticism, xiii, 39–40, 113
redaction, 15–16
reference, 16
reversal, 8, 11, 75–77, 79, 96
rewritten Bible, 4, 13–14

Satan, 69, 85, 87–88, 101, 107–9, 149, 151
Sevius, 30
source criticism, xiv
style, 52

Thomas, Gospel of, 46
Torah, 4
Troy, 11, 68
Two-Source Hypothesis, xiii

universalization, 7

variation, 6, 110, 112, 151, 153
Virgil, 7–12, 29–30, 50, 69

Ancient Document Index

OLD TESTAMENT/HEBREW BIBLE

Genesis
1:2	68
24:11–21	128

Exodus
2:16	128
12:1–29	133
12:14	135
24:1–8	133
24:18	86

Leviticus
18:16	102
20:21	102

Deuteronomy
2:33	139
25:5	102
29:10–11	128

Joshua
9:21–27	128
10:8	139

Judges
8:3	139

First Samuel
9:11	128
10:1–10	128
10:1	122, 127
17:47	139

First Kings
18:12	86
18:20–40	89
18:20–21	89
18:27	89
18:30	89
18:36–39	89
19:2	102
19:5–8	86
19:15–18	82, 85
19:19–21	73, 77

Second Kings
1:8	78
2	78
2:6	86
4:9	89
5:10	78
5:14	78
9:3	122
9:6	122, 128

Nehemiah
13:14	122
13:22	122

Ancient Document Index

Esther
2:9	103

Psalms
2:7	68
10:7–8	121
41:9	139

Isaiah
1:2	64
53:6	133
53:10	139
53:12	133
61:1–2	67–68

Hosea
6:2	121

Zechariah
9:11	133
14:9	133

Malachi
1:1	64
3:1	61
3:22	61

APOCRYPHA

First Esdras
1:17	122

Four Maccabees
17:8	122

PSEUDEPIGRAPHA

Joseph and Aseneth
8–21	117
14:1–3	28

NEW TESTAMENT

Mark
1–8	45
1:1–28	53, 55–99, 107, 149–50, 152–53
1:1–15	58
1:1–13	58
1:1–8	57–58
1:1–3	48, 56–66, 68, 83, 95
1:1	61, 70
1:2–3	67, 79
1:2	61–62
1:4–8	53, 56, 58–59, 77–81, 149
1:4	58, 79
1:8	79
1:9–11	56, 59, 66–72
1:9	95, 99
1:10–11	70
1:10	28, 67–68
1:11	68, 70–2
1:12–13	56, 59, 85–88, 149
1:13	58, 87
1:14–15	56, 59, 81–85
1:14	64, 71
1:15	83–84
1:16–20	56, 59, 72–77, 90, 94, 149
1:18	75, 129–30
1:19	76, 95
1:21–28	56, 59, 88–92, 95, 150
1:21–22	89, 91
1:21	89
1:23–26	89, 91
1:23	89
1:24	89–91
1:26	89
1:27–28	89, 91
1:28	58
1:29	58
2:12	58
3:5	44
4:1–34	38
4:21	62
5:24–34	105
6:6	102
6:14–29	52–53, 100–112, 150, 153
6:14	108
6:30–44	53

6:53	44
7:1–23	39
7:21–23	44
7:21–22	111
7:24–30	105
8	106
8:1–9	53
8:17	44
8:21	102
9:13	62
10:1–12	53
10:38–39	43, 80
10:41–45	42
10:45	42, 43
12:13–17	43
13:1—14:11	122
14–16	121
14	113
14:1–25	53, 113–47, 151, 153
14:1–11	119–28, 139
14:1	118, 121–22, 134, 138
14:3–9	124
14:3	125
14:4	124–25, 143, 151
14:9	122, 124
14:12–21	132
14:12–16	119, 126–31
14:12	119, 129, 138
14:13	129
14:14	129
14:17–21	119, 138–42
14:17	115, 134
14:21	133
14:22–25	39, 53, 119, 131–38, 145, 152
14:22	132, 136–37
14:23	136–37
14:24–25	132
14:24	137
14:25	118, 133, 136–37
14:26	114, 118

John

13:30	115

Acts

13:13	34
15:36–41	34

Romans

1:1–7	48
1:1–3	62
1:1	61
1:29–31	44
6:16–23	42
8:14–22	70
9–11	38
11:7	44
13:1–7	44
13:12	82

First Corinthians

1–2	53, 55–99, 107, 144, 149–50, 152
1:1–3	55, 59–66, 95
1:2	64
1:4–9	55, 57, 59, 66–72
1:4–7	70
1:4	71–72
1:7	70
1:8	71, 95, 99
1:9	70–71
1:10–17	56–57
1:10–13	55, 57, 59, 63, 72–77, 94, 149
1:10	75–6, 95, 129–30
1:14–17	53, 56, 59, 77–81, 149
1:14–16	57
1:14	56–57, 83
1:17	57, 79, 81
1:18–25	56–57, 59, 81–85, 97
1:18	83
1:19	63
1:20	83
1:21	62
1:26–31	56, 59, 83, 85–88, 90, 149
1:31	63
2	57, 59, 86, 88–92, 94–95, 150
2:1–5	56–57, 89, 91
2:2	91
2:6–16	56–57
2:6–9	89, 91
2:6	57
2:9	62
2:10–6	89, 91
2:13	91
4	55

167

Ancient Document Index

First Corinthians (*continued*)

5	52–53, 100–112, 150, 153
5:1	108
5:5	109, 151
5:6–8	108, 110–11
5:7	114
5:11	110
6	100
7–15	118
7	88
7:1–16	53
7:5	87, 149
8:1—11:1	118
8:1–13	53
10:14—11:1	53
11:2–34	53, 106, 113–47, 151, 153
11:2–16	119–26
11:2	118, 131, 134
11:16	124, 143, 151
11:17–22	119, 126–31
11:17–19	129
11:18	129
11:20–22	129
11:23–26	39, 53, 119, 131–38, 145, 153
11:23	115, 118, 136, 144
11:24	124, 131, 136–37
11:25	132, 137
11:26	125, 137
11:27–34	119, 138–42
12:1—14:40	118
12:7–11	70

Second Corinthians

3:14	44
13:11	76

Galatians

4:6	70
5:22	70

Colossians

1:13	82
4:10	34

First Thessalonians

5:5–6	82

Second Timothy

4:11	34

Philemon

1:24	34

First Peter

5:12–13	34

Second Peter

3:15–16	92

GRECO-ROMAN WRITINGS

Apollonius Rhodius

Argonautica

2:1–97	9

Homer

Iliad

23:653–99	9

Odyssey

5	11
10.100–3	128
10.105–16	128
10.476–560	117, 134
18.66	9
19	122

Isocrates

Panegyricus

7–8	6

Lucan

De Bello Civili

1.685–86	29

Quintilian

Institutio Oratoria

1.9.2	5
10.1.1	3

10.2.1–2		7	1:257–96		11
			1:657–94		11
Virgil			3:557–58		30
Aeneid			5:424		9
			11:59–99		12
1:12–33		11			

www.ingramcontent.com/pod-product-compliance
Lightning Source LLC
Chambersburg PA
CBHW052059230426
43662CB00036B/1702